STRANGE
SCOTTISH STORIES

Retold and Illustrated
by William Owen

Jarrold Publishing, Norwich

Introduction

Stories of the supernatural always fascinate, and such stories are nowhere more popular or more numerous than in the Highlands of Scotland where there is a long tradition of story-telling. No one is more welcome at a Highland fireside than he who can tell a strange story or two. Most Highland tales are based on historical incidents, but in the telling they have become embroidered with more than a little superstition (often in an attempt to explain the inexplicable). In this world of myth and legend the blame for evil acts and strange happenings is frequently firmly placed on such supernatural beings as fairies, kelpies and, of course, Satan himself. When the wrongdoers are human, these 'baddies' are often factors, landowners, murderers and recruiting officers, categories of people who have been guilty of persecuting the Highlanders over the years. In these stories the evil ones always get their just deserts; if not in life, then certainly after death.

I have adapted and abridged some stories where they were too long for this volume and, when I thought fit, put them into more modern language. I have also taken the liberty of introducing dialogue in places when no record of the dialogue exists, and where I felt that it would add life to the text.

Contents

THE LAST SEAFORTH 4

SEVEN BLOODY HEADS 14

THE FAIRIES OF TOMNAHURICH 20

THE APPIN MURDER 28

THE ANOINTED MAN 40

THE BLACK CAPTAIN 46

THE WIDOW'S CURSE 58

THE WATER KELPIE OF LOCH NESS 72

THE TREACHEROUS BARBARA 80

A WEE BIT PROPERTY 88

VENGEANCE OF THE SPIRITS 98

FORECAST OF DEATH 104

THE STORY OF SANDY WOOD 118

RODERICK MACKENZIE 126

AS SURE AS DEATH 134

THE LAST SEAFORTH

The Last Seaforth

When scarlet fever swept through the boys' boarding-school some of the boys were sent home but others who had taken the infection, those who lived too far away to return home, were moved into a large room to be treated. One evening after the attendant nurse had left the room, one of the patients, a twelve-year-old boy, saw the door opposite his bed begin to open. Slowly and silently a hideous old woman entered the room. She had a wallet containing some large object hanging from her neck in front of her. She paused on entering, then turned to the bed nearest the door and stared steadily at the boy lying in it. She then passed to the foot of the next boy's bed and, after a moment, stealthily moved up to the head. From the wallet hung around her neck she took a mallet and a wooden peg. She held the peg to the head of the sleeping boy and with one swift blow of the mallet drove the peg into his forehead. Frozen with terror, the watching boy could only stare wide-eyed, his jaw tightly locked and his breathing suspended. The old hag proceeded round the room looking at each boy in turn. She paused longer at some beds than at others. At some she would again reach into the wallet, take out a peg and the watching boy would hear the sickening crunch of the bone as she drove the peg deep into the forehead of the unfortunate child.

As he watched the hag work her way around the beds and approach nearer and nearer to his own, his suspense was awful. At last she came to him. She stood at the foot of his bed, her staring eyes upon his face. He saw her move to his side and reach into the wallet, but still he felt that he could not move or cry out. Paralysed with fear he waited for the blow but it never came; instead he felt her cold, bony fingers touch his ears. Eventually she began to move away and after completing her circuit of the room she went out by the same door she had entered. As it closed behind her it was as if a spell had been lifted from the boy, and he found his voice in a scream which brought the nurse running into the room. She discovered him in a great state of excitement and totally incoherent, but eventually he became calm enough to tell her what he had seen. She immediately examined the other children but finding them unharmed she laughed at his story and told him that he'd had a nightmare.

When the doctor came an hour later to make his rounds, he observed that the boy was feverish and excited, and afterwards he asked the nurse if she knew the cause, whereupon she reported what had occurred. The doctor, struck with the story, returned to the boy's bedside and made him repeat his dream which he wrote down just as the boy had told him.

In course of time some of the boys died; some suffered but slightly, while others, though they recovered, bore some evil trace and consequence of the fever for the rest of their lives. The doctor to his horror found that those whom the boy had described as having a peg driven into their foreheads were those who died from the fever; those whom the hag passed by recovered and were none the worse; whereas those she appeared to stare at intently or handle, all suffered afterwards. The boy who had seen the vision was the young Lord Seaforth. He left his bed of sickness almost stone-deaf and in later years he also lost his powers of speech.

His affliction had been forecast many years earlier by a remarkable Seer, one Kenneth Mackenzie, better known as Coinneach Odhar or the Brahan Seer. The gift of prophecy, or Second Sight as it is commonly called in the Highlands, is popularly believed to be a faculty of prophetic vision. A person possessing this gift is supposed, without any previous knowledge, to see into the future at a distance of both time and place and consequently can foretell death or accident and many other events. This psychic power is not confined to the Scottish Highlands. In one or other of its forms it has been found among Australian Aborigines, Aztecs, Incas, Maoris, Polynesians, Greeks and Egyptians and many other peoples.

The Second Sight is, in every case, regarded as troublesome to the possessor. The vision of coming events is attended by a 'nerve-storm' which leaves the subject of it in a state of complete prostration. Hence, it is not an enviable gift. The Second Sight may excite the surprise and the incredulity of the learned, but of its existence, even in some Highlanders to the present day, there is not the shadow of a doubt in the minds of many. There may not today be the same faculty of foretelling events in the more distant future, as in one or two of the Brahan Seer's trustworthy forecasts, but among Highlanders generally the existence of the gift is regarded as an indisputable fact, and in almost every one of the more rural communities there are one or more persons who are known to have the power of 'seeing'.

From all accounts it appears that the Brahan Seer was born at Baille-na-Cille, Uig, in the Island of Lewis, and that his prophecies were uttered between the years 1630 and 1679. Having been born on the Seaforth property in Lewis, he became known to the Lord Seaforth of the day as one who possessed the gift of Second Sight, and no doubt because of this he was not only employed on the estate but became a favourite of the family. In his early manhood he removed to the neighbourhood of Brahan Castle on the mainland and became a frequent visitor to the castle. Being possessed of a ready wit, he was even at times admitted to the company of the castle parties.

There are two traditional accounts of how the Seer came to make the Seaforth prophecy and one of them refers to his attendance at one of the castle parties. On the occasion of a convivial gathering at which many Highland gentry were present, the younger members were amusing themselves in the beautiful grounds surrounding the castle and displaying their noble forms and features, as they thought to full advantage when a party remarked in Coinneach Odhar's hearing that such a gathering of gentlemen's children could rarely be seen. The Seer answered scornfully 'I see more in the company of footmen and grooms than of the children of gentlemen.' This remark soon came to the ears of Lady Seaforth and the other ladies present, who were so much offended and provoked at this insult that they determined at once to have the Seer punished. On the same traditional authority we have another reason why Lady Seaforth sought to have the Seer punished. It appears that her husband – the third Earl – was absent for some time in Paris soon after the Restoration of Charles II. He was not too dutiful in his remembrance of those he had left behind at Brahan, and the Countess chafed under the thought of his continued silence and his possible doings among the gay Parisians. In her distress she called for the Seer, knowing that he might be able to divine something of his whereabouts and doings. In due time the Seer appeared before the Countess at the Castle of Brahan, and the traditional account of the interview is as follows:

The Seer asked where Seaforth was supposed to be and on being told, he said to the Countess, 'Fear not for your lord, he is safe and sound, well and hearty, merry and happy. Be satisfied,' he continued, 'ask no questions. Let it suffice you to know that your lord is well and merry.'

'But,' demanded the lady, 'where is he? With whom is he? And is he making any preparations for coming home?'

'Your lord,' replied the Seer, 'is in a magnificent room in very fine company and far too agreeably employed at present to think of leaving Paris.'

The Countess, however, thought there was something odd about the Seer's looks and her suspicions were aroused. He had spoken sneeringly of her husband's occupations, as much as to say that he could tell a disagreeable tale if he wished. The lady tried entreaties, bribes and threats to induce the Seer to give a true account of her husband's doings, at which the Seer pulled himself up and proceeded to say: 'As you will know that which will make you unhappy, I must tell you the truth. My lord seems to have little thought of you, of his children or of his Highland home. I saw him in a gaily gilded room, grandly decked out in velvet, silks and cloth of gold, and on his knees before a fair lady, his arm round her waist and her hand pressed to his lips.'

At this unexpected disclosure, the rage of the lady knew no bounds, but she vented her anger on the Seer and not on the erring husband, because the Seer had told his tale in the presence of the principal retainers of her house, so that the Earl's desertion of her for a French lady was certain to become a public scandal. She formed a sudden resolution and with equal presence of mind and cruelty turned to the Seer and said, 'You have spoken evil of dignitaries; you have vilified the mighty of the land; you have defamed a mighty chief in the midst of his vassals; you have abused my hospitality and outraged my feelings; you have sullied the good name of my lord in the halls of his ancestors; and you shall suffer the death.'

Coinneach, filled with astonishment and dismay, could not at first believe the rage of the Countess to be serious. At all events, he expected that in the course of a few hours he would be allowed to depart in peace. But the decision of the Countess was no less violently conceived than it was promptly executed. The doom of the Seer was sealed. Kenneth Odhar was, accordingly, charged before the Presbytery of Chanonry with trafficking with the Devil. In those days sorcery was considered the most serious of crimes and, even when there was no powerful lady to accuse, suspicion was usually held to be sufficient evidence of the fact. The Seer's conviction was a foregone conclusion. He was taken to

Chanonry Point where with unrelenting severity the stern army of ecclesiastical authority had him burned to death by being thrown head first into a barrel of blazing tar.

When Coinneach Odhar was being led to the place of execution fast bound with cords, he delivered the following prediction:

'I see a Chief, the last of his House, both deaf and dumb. He will be the father of four fair sons, all of whom he shall follow to the tomb. He shall live careworn and die mourning, knowing that the honours of his House are to be extinguished forever, and that no future Chief of the Mackenzies shall rule in Kintail. After lamenting over the last and most promising of his sons, he himself shall sink into the grave, and the remnant of his possessions shall be inherited by a white-coiffed lassie from the East; and she shall kill her sister. As a sign by which it shall be known that these things are coming to pass, there shall be four great lairds in the days of the last Seaforth, one of whom shall be buck-toothed, the second hare-lipped, the third half-witted, and the fourth a stammerer. Seaforth, when he looks round and sees them, may know that his sons are doomed to death, and that his broad lands shall come to an end.'

The long and romantic story of the fulfilment of the Seaforth prediction has often been told. On the death of the last Seaforth it was detailed in practically the whole Press of this country. *The Edinburgh Daily Review* had a particularly well-informed account. After giving an outline of the family history of the Seaforths and describing how the fifth Earl embraced the losing side in the rising of 1715, it recounted his fighting at the head of his clan at Sheriffmuir and how in 1719 he, along with the Marquess of Tullibardine and the Earl Marischal, made a final attempt to bring the 'auld Stewarts back again'. He was dangerously wounded in an encounter with the Government forces at Glenshiel and was compelled to abandon the vain enterprise. He was then carried on board a vessel by his clansmen, conveyed to the Western Isles, and ultimately to France. Shortly afterwards he was attainted by Parliament and his estates forfeited to the Crown.

Despite all the efforts of the Government, Officers of the Crown failed to penetrate into Kintail or to collect any rent from his faithful Macraes, whom the Seaforths had so often led victorious from many a bloody conflict, from the Battle of Largs down to the Jacobite Risings of 1715 and 1719. The rents of that part of the estates were regularly collected and remitted to their exiled chief in France with a devotion and faithfulness only to be equalled by their own countrymen when their beloved 'Bonnie Prince Charlie' was a wanderer, helpless and forlorn, and at the mercies of his enemies.

The article continues: 'But the Seaforths' downfall came at last, and the failure of the male line of this great historical family was attended with circumstances as singular as they were painful. Francis, Lord Seaforth, the last Baron of Kintail, was (says Sir Walter Scott), "a nobleman of extraordinary talents who must have made for himself a lasting reputation had not his political exertions been checked by painful natural infirmity." Though deaf, and inflicted also with a partial impediment of speech, he was distinguished for his attainments as well as for his intellectual ability. He represented Ross-shire in Parliament for a number of years and was later Lord-Lieutenant of the county. During the Revolutionary War with France, he raised a splendid regiment of Ross-shire Highlanders (the 78th; the second which had been raised among his clan) of which he was appointed Lieutenant-Colonel Commandant. He ultimately attained the rank of Lieutenant-General in the Army. For six years he was Governor of Barbados and, through being firm and just, succeeded in putting an end to the practice of killing slaves. At that time this was not infrequent in the island and was deemed by the planters a trivial matter to be punished by a small fine. Lord Seaforth was the father of four sons and six daughters, all of high promise; and it seemed as if he were destined to raise the illustrious house of which he was the head to a height of honour and power greater than it had ever yet attained. But when he saw his four sons, three of them rising to man's estate, and when he looked around him and observed the peculiar marks set upon the persons of the four contemporary Highland lairds – all in strict accordance with Coinneach's prophecy – he must have felt ill at ease, unless with the incredulous indifference of a man of the world he was able to spurn the Seer's predictions as old wives' superstitions.

'The closing years of this nobleman were darkened by calamities. The mismanagement of his estates in the West Indies caused him many difficulties and compelled him to dispose of a part of his Kintail estates – "the gift-land of the family", as it was termed – a step which his tenantry and clansmen endeavoured to avert by offering to buy the land for him so that it might not pass from the family. At the time that Kintail was sold, three of his sons were dead. His only remaining son, a young man of talent and eloquence, was the representative in Parliament of his native county when he suddenly died too. The broken-hearted father lingered on for a few months, his fine intellect enfeebled by paralysis, and yet, as Sir Walter Scott says, "not so entirely obscured but that he perceived his deprivation as in a glass, darkly."'

Thus the whole story conforms in remarkable detail with the Brahan Seer's prediction that there should be a deaf and dumb Chief of the clan; that the 'gift-land' of their territory would be sold, and the male line become extinct. The chiefdom of the Mackenzies, divested of its rank and honour, passed away to a very remote collateral who succeeded to no portion of the property, and the great Seaforth estates were inherited by 'a white-hooded lassie' from the East, Lord Seaforth's eldest surviving daughter, the Hon. Mary Frederica Elizabeth Mackenzie. In 1804 she had married Admiral Sir Samuel Hood of the West India Station when Seaforth himself was Governor in those islands. Sir Samuel afterwards had the chief command in the Indian seas, whither his lady accompanied him, and she spent several years with him in different parts of the East Indies. He died while holding that high command, very nearly at the same time as Lord Seaforth, so that his youthful wife was a recent widow at the time and returned home from India in her widow's weeds to take possession of her paternal inheritance. She was thus literally a white-coiffed or white-hooded lassie (that is, a young woman in widow's weeds, and a Hood by name) from the East.

After some years of widowhood, Lady Hood Mackenzie married a second time. Her husband was a Stewart, grandson of the sixth Earl of Galloway, who assumed the name of Mackenzie and established himself on his lady's extensive estates in the north. Thus, the possessions of Seaforth may truly be said to have passed from the male line of the ancient House of Mackenzie. And still more strikingly was the prophecy fulfilled when Mr and Mrs Stewart Mackenzie sold the great Island of Lewis to Sir James Matheson.

After many years of happiness and prosperity, a frightful accident happened and once again the family was in mourning. One day Mrs Stewart Mackenzie was driving her younger sister, the Hon. Caroline Mackenzie, in a pony carriage. As they drove among the woods in the vicinity of Brahan Castle the ponies suddenly took fright and started off at a furious pace; Mrs Stewart Mackenzie was quite unable to check them, and both she and her sister were thrown out of the carriage and injured. Happily Mrs Stewart Mackenzie soon recovered from the accident, but the injury which her sister sustained proved fatal, and after lingering for some time in a hopeless state, she died. As Mrs

Stewart Mackenzie was driving the carriage at the time of the accident, she may be said to have been the innocent cause of her sister's death and thus completed the Coinneach's prophecy.

Original Sources: *Highland Second Sight* by Norman Macrae, 1908: *The Prophecies of the Brahan Seer* by Alexander Mackenzie, 1878; *The Edinburgh Daily Review*.

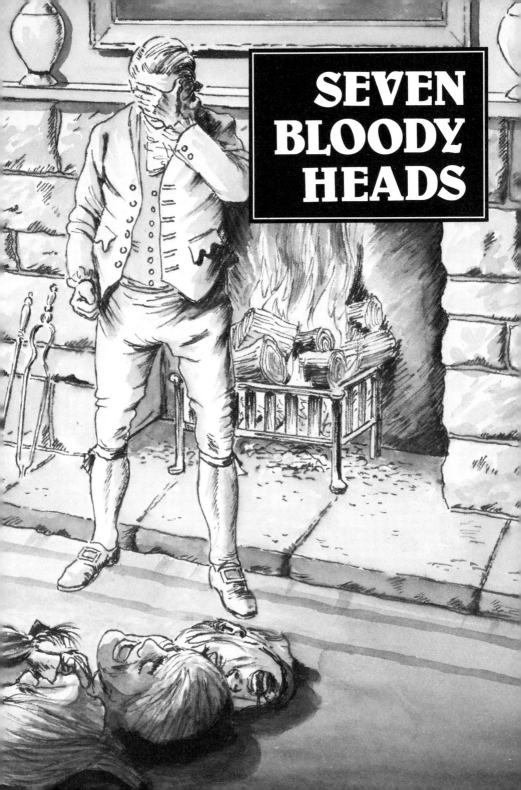

SEVEN BLOODY HEADS

Seven Bloody Heads

Close beside the road on the shores of Loch Oich stands an unusual monument which has the name *Tobar nan Ceann* or 'The Well of the Seven Heads'. On the top of the monument, sculptured in stone, is a hand holding seven heads transfixed by a dagger. It commemorates a barbarous crime and an equally barbarous retribution.

This is Macdonell country. The Macdonells of Glengarry are a branch of the powerful Clan Donald, so, too, are the Macdonalds of Keppoch, whose lands lie some miles to the south on the other side of Loch Lochy. The crime involved both of these branches of Clan Donald for, although the murders took place in Keppoch territory, Glengarry held the title 'Superior of Clan Donald' and as such he had the authority to bring the wrongdoers to justice.

The victims of this crime which was perpetrated about the year 1663, were the two sons of Donald Glas, the eleventh Chief of the Macdonalds of Keppoch. At the time of their father's death from natural causes, these two young men were at school on the Continent where they had been sent to be educated and prepared for the positions they would have to fill at the head of the Keppoch Clan. Immediately upon the death of old Keppoch seven relatives of the absent heirs assumed control of the estates and enjoyed the power and increased wealth that this brought them. The arrival from the Continent of the two youthful chiefs soon put an end to their aggrandizement, and they plotted together to rid themselves of their young kinsmen at the earliest opportunity.

One night the head of one of the lesser branches of the Clan Keppoch, together with his six sons, set out from their home at Inverlair and after wading the River Spean below Keppoch Castle quietly entered the castle and plunged their dirks into the eldest of the two chiefs as he lay in his bed. His brother Ranald, who happened to be outside the castle, heard the commotion and ran inside, only to be instantly seized. Seeing his uncle Alastair Buidhe among the company he called to him for help, but the uncle, intending rather to help him into the next world, was the first to bury his dirk in his nephew's heart. The other conspirators followed suit before fleeing back to their home at Inverlair.

When news of the murders reached Iain Lom, the Bard of Keppoch, he vowed a terrible oath of vengeance against the assassins, even though they were the sons of his own sister. The Bard swore never to rest until those guilty of this crime were brought to justice. Strangely enough, there were no such strong feelings among other members of the clan. As the two young chiefs had been absent abroad for a long time and on their return introduced unpopular measures such as discouraging cattle-lifting by their clansmen, in a country where such pursuits were a way of life, such policies were particularly unpopular. The Bard, finding that he could not rouse them from their apathy, applied to Macdonell of Glengarry, a distant relative of the murdered youths, whom he presumed would be passionately interested in seeing the murderers brought to justice. Glengarry, however, was reluctant to interfere in the affairs of another branch of the clan. Indignant at this, Iain Lom decided to appeal to another chieftain of Clan Donald, Sir Alexander MacDonald of Sleat. The Bard received a better reception from this chief and a promise that he would send sufficient men into Glen Spean to enable Iain Lom to fulfil his vow.

The family of assassins expected an avenging party to come from Glengarry and they kept a watch in that direction from the summit of a near-by hill. But Iain Lom outwitted them by approaching Inverlair from another direction. The family had fortified their home, but the islemen made a determined attack and soon forced an entrance. The sons were dragged outside and slain and the house was set on fire. At first the father could not be found, and Iain Lom called to his companions, 'The six cubs are here, but the old fox is still in the den.' A search was made, and the old man was soon found and he met the same fate as his sons. Iain Lom used a dirk to sever the heads from the bodies, and putting them into a sack he carried them to Invergarry where he stopped at a small spring beside Loch Oich in order to wash his gory trophies. Today the spring is marked by the monument *Tobar nan Ceann*. After washing the heads Iain Lom went on to Glengarry Castle where he presented them to the Chief and taunted him for not having

17

taken any part in bringing the murderers of his kinsmen to justice.

Sometime in the nineteenth century an antiquarian in Fort William sought to discover if all the details of the tradition were true. He dug into the mound at Inverlair where the bodies were said to have been buried and there he found seven skeletons which were complete except for their skulls.

There can be little doubt that the Scriptural vengeance of 'an eye for an eye, and a tooth for a tooth' was taken literally in the Highlands in those days, for many are the traditional stories told of grizzly revenge and dark deeds bloodily done.

THE FAIRIES OF TOMNAHURICH

The Fairies
of Tomnahurich

A mile westward of the town of Inverness there rises out of a perfectly flat plain a very regular hill, its curious shape presenting the appearance of a huge ship with the keel uppermost. It rises about two hundred and fifty feet above the level of the River Ness: it is almost two thousand feet in length and has a breadth of about a hundred and seventy-five feet. The hill within recent years has become a cemetery laid out with terraced walks. The view from the plateau at the top commands a varied panorama of mountain, valley, town and the distant Moray Firth.

For ages Tomnahurich has been thought of as being a '*sithein dun*' or 'fairy hillock'. Mounds of this kind in Scotland and especially in the Highlands have from time immemorial been associated with those diminutive beings called *daoine shi* or 'fairies'. The following story has been passed down through many generations of Invernessians:

Long ago – so all stories of fairies begin – there came to Inverness two wandering Highland fiddlers, Farquhar Grant and Thomas Cumming, natives of that famous strath which gave birth to those sprightly dances called Strathspeys that delight the true Highlander. Farquhar and Thomas were compelled by the failure of the crops and consequently the slackness of business in their native musical strath, to pay a visit to the *baile mor* or 'great town' to raise some funds for the maintenance of themselves and their families left behind them.

They arrived in Inverness one frosty evening near Christmas-time. Proceeding along East Street (now the modern High Street of the town) to the top of Bridge Street, where were then situated the better-class buildings, they started to play their most favourite airs. Although they plied their bows with great skill and dexterity, the townspeople passed on, taking no heed of their most celebrated performances or if they stood, it was to listen without rewarding their labours. Still they kept on playing till their fingers were becoming quite numb with the sharp cutting frost that prevailed. Eventually the passers-by became fewer till, like the hopes and expectations of the two fiddlers, all had faded away. Our two friends were further aggravated by the rich fragrance of the evening's meal which met them as they passed down Bridge Street and they wished themselves back again in their native strath, blaming themselves for coming to a place where their merits seemed to be unappreciated.

In this hopeless and despairing condition they reached the bottom of the street, where stood the old baronial building called Castle Tolmie with its curious pepperbox turrets and turnpike staircases. (This building was pulled down in 1854 to make room for the approach to the new Suspension Bridge over the River Ness.) From under the shadow of Castle Tolmie, they saw approach them an old man with a venerable appearance, whose tranquil countenance betokened a heart of benevolence and promised that they might at last receive some reward for their talents so unappreciated by the other citizens of Inverness. With a familiarity that assumed a knowledge of who they were and from whence they came, he addressed them.

'Well, how do matters go with you and all other old friends at Tullochgorum?' Looking somewhat surprised at this enquiry from the old man, who was a complete stranger to them, they respectfully replied –

'Poorly enough, sir.'

'Aye', quoth the old man, with a long-drawn sigh, 'it misses our good folks now; but', he continued, 'you are in want of employment in your profession, and we are in want of music, which I know you can well give us; so come along with me.'

The two musicians, glad at the prospect of earning some money that they so much needed, were loud in their expressions of gratitude and thanks to the old man. They quickly and cheerfully put their instruments into their bags and followed the old man who with rapid strides had proceeded to cross the river by the old oak bridge that stood across the Ness. (This bridge which fell in 1644, was described as 'the weakest that ever straddled so strong a stream'. It had an arched passage, which passed through a portion of Castle Tolmie, and served as a gateway to defend the entrance to the town from that approach. The two fiddlers arrived almost breathless on the west bank of the river.

The old man, still preceding them, with equal haste as before, turned to enquire, 'Are you coming, friends?'

'We are doing our best, sir,' said one of the panting fiddlers, 'but, my faith, you fairly beat us.'

'Move quicker, Farquhar of Feshie,' cried the old man, 'our people will be getting impatient for our arrival.'

'Preserve us, Farquhar,' rejoined the other fiddler, 'but the gentleman kens us whatever.'

'Aye, and you too, Tom-an-Torran,' continued the old man.

By this time they had passed by the few low Highland huts that stood at that period near where Tomnahurich Street is now built, and while they stumbled across the rough unploughed land where whin, broom, and stones were the chief crops, the old man skipped and leaped with great agility so that he reached the base of Tomnahurich Hill well before them. No sooner had they arrived there than the old man, still in advance, began to ascend the hill, but the two fiddlers, who, besides being out of breath, had by this time begun to feel sundry misgivings with respect to their conductor, hesitated, but only for a moment, when they felt themselves impelled on up the hillside as if by some power, they knew not how, till at last they landed on a small grassless plateau half-way up the side of Tomnahurich. Here they observed the old man beat with his foot on the ground and wave his hand as if inviting them to precede him. They stepped forward into the shadows which seemed to close about them until ahead of them brilliant lights appeared and they found themselves entering a palatial hall filled with lights so dazzling that they were bewildered. Farquhar turned to his companion as if he wished to address him but was unable, only he mentally declared that Castle Grant with all its feudal surroundings was as nothing compared with the splendour to which the old man had just introduced them.

Glancing round, the two fiddlers saw tables, as they thought of pure diamond, placed in niches of crystal around the vast hall, and these tables were profusely laden with viands, fruits, and liquors of every description that the bewildered Strathspey men knew not the name of. The walls of the room appeared as a mirrored sheet reflecting a thousandfold the various objects, while the arched roof seemed to them as a sky of burnished gold supported by fluted columns and pillars sparkling with countless precious stones. They had not spent much time looking at this vision of splendour when the hall was filled with hundreds of figures – diminutive, it is true, but light, young and lovely forms which glided before them in ever-changing circles and groups. they looked on but for a moment at the strange scene passing before them when they were invitingly addressed by several of those graceful beings.

'Farquhar o' Feshie and Tom-an-Torran, come, eat, drink, and be merry; do not put off any time, begin and satisfy your wants.'

The fiddlers, delighted, accepted the invitation thus given them and began to do full justice to the good things before them. They ate and drank until they could eat and drink no more. So busy were they that they did not observe that no matter how much they ate there was no diminution of the quantity of the eatables spread out so temptingly before them. At last they appeared to have satisfied their wants and they were then invited to take their place on a slightly elevated platform on the opposite side of the hall from where they had partaken of their repast, and they were called upon to begin to play, which they did.

And now began the dance. The musicians had seen many dances in their professional experience, light, bright, and graceful, but Farquhar afterwards avowed that the fairest and nimblest of the daughters of any laird on Speyside fell as far short of the beauty and grace of this assemblage as his old mother at Glenfeshie might have done of the proud and stately lady of Castle Grant. Strathspeys, reels and jigs flew on with the rapidity of lightning, but the catgut never snapped, nor did the bow require rosin. Time was certainly flying on the wings of the wind as they played fast and furious, but to the fiddlers it seemed impossible to say or conjecture how the hours sped on. The happy musicians were plied with liquor in which they pledged the lovely company of dancers. In the midst of their joy, however, the old man who had engaged them in the Bridge Street of Inverness suddenly appeared. They had lost sight of him since they entered on this scene of pleasure till now. He told them that the morning was considerably advanced and that the music must now cease.

'Come,' said he 'attend, and I will lead you to the entrance door of our mansion, and I shall pay you for your night's exertions to the full content of your hearts.'

Reluctantly did the fiddlers put up their instruments and lingeringly followed the old man through the hall, while they also observed that the agile and gay dancers had as quickly disappeared from the scene.

When they reached the entrance of this strange mansion, the old man turned and said, 'Now, Farquhar of Feshie, and you, good Tom-an-

Torran, extend the palms of your hands and receive payment for your services to our people.'

An order which the Strathspey men readily obeyed, when to their surprise he placed in each of their hands a purse filled with gold.

'Are you satisfied with your night's work, friends?' enquired the old man.

'Satisfied!' quoth Tom-an-Torran. 'Heaven bless you and your people!'

But the benediction of the grateful fiddler was bestowed on the air, for the old man had disappeared from their sight, and the musicians found themselves alone on the sloping side of Tomnahurich.

With feelings of wonder they set off down the hill to make their way back to the town of Inverness which they had left, as they supposed, the night before. Their surprise at the old man's sudden disappearance was not lessened by the sights that now met their eyes as they walked along. Where there had been the rough and uncultivated land they had passed over the previous night there now appeared fields of waving corn; while near approaching the town they had to pass through a street of well-built houses.

On reaching the river, they found, instead of the tumbledown oak bridge, a finely built stone one of seven arches. 'Tis true that old Castle Tolmie still stood on the spot as they had seen it when they had made their engagement with the stranger, but the street and the surrounding buildings had all undergone some change. Inverness, to every appearance, had advanced in all directions. The citizens that walked its streets were clothed differently, while even their very language was altered.

They addressed the people they met and enquired how all this came to be, and their questions were answered with a laugh or a doubtful shake of the head. Many jeered at their appearance and the strange enquiries they made, till at last, as they continued questioning and telling their story, they came to be looked upon as lunatics or imposters seeking to deceive the inhabitants.

They left the town in disgust, and with weary footsteps made their way back to their native strath. But alas! they found the district had undergone a change. They knew not the people they found there, nor were they known by the dwellers therein. The very hamlets where dwelt their kindred they could not find. The poor fiddlers now became more astonished than ever and began to look upon themselves as bewitched, and as a last resort strayed to their parish church.

As they approached the church, sacred to them by many associations, they observed that even here the hand of change had attacked the old edifice that they so well knew, and that it had been enlarged and altered from what they remembered it before leaving their native strath. In passing through the churchyard to the house of God, they stopped to search for the graves where their kindred had been buried, and to their grief found that names had been added to those cut on the stones of this last resting-place – these new names were those of their wives and children who had been dead for a century or more.

They now entered the church at last, but only to find here the pulpit occupied by a strange minster they knew not. They stood in amazement near the doorway but failed to recognise any face among those who were seated near them. The poor fiddlers and the congregation were alike unknowing and unknown.

No sooner had the clergyman opened the Bible and given forth the chapter and begun the reading of the Sacred Word and coming to the name of God, than the two musicians, who had been standing near the doorway and who were stared at by the people as oddities from their antique dress and old-world appearance, were observed by the congregation to suddenly disappear from their sight, crumbling into dust before their eyes.

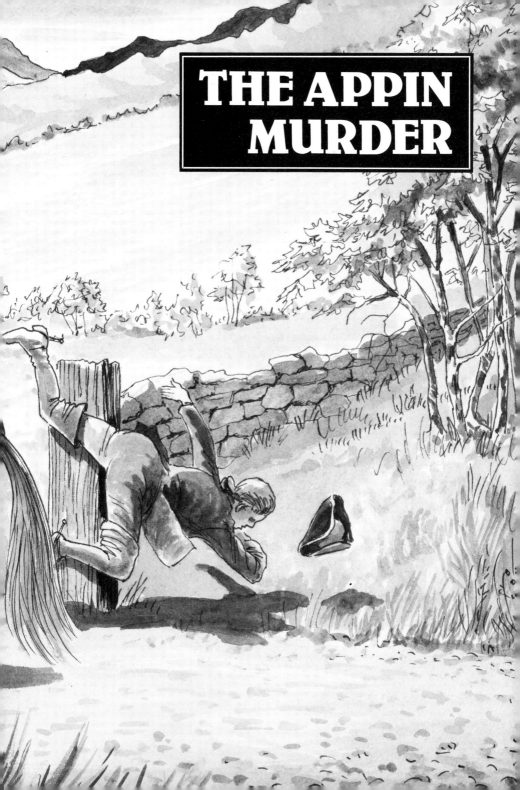

THE APPIN MURDER

The Appin Murder

Barbarism is a monster which, it seems, man is incapable of killing. A monster which rears its ugly head from time to time, in this place or that, wherever mankind dwells. Certainly it made its evil presence felt in the Highlands at the time to which I refer. The hardships endured by those Highlanders on the losing side after the Jacobite Risings of 1715, 1719 and 1745 are well known. There was a great deal of barbarity and when one considers the cruel treatment meted out to the Highlanders by the Hanoverians, it is surprising that so few clansmen ever attempted to take revenge upon their oppressors. Perhaps the best-known instance is the Appin Murder. This murder, which has never been satisfactorily solved, took place in 1752 in Appin, a district of Argyll.

When writing or speaking of it one hesitates to use the word 'murder' because this was murder only in the strictly legal sense. The man who died was an evil oppressor of the people, and many in the district sincerely felt that he deserved his fate. The killer was not simply seeking personal revenge. He was encouraged and supported and no doubt believed that in ridding the country of this evil man he was serving his people. He might have felt no more compunction in killing this man that he would in killing a mad dog. No other murder in Scotland's history has been the subject of so much discussion and speculation, not only at the time it took place but down to the present day. For it seems that although only one man did the actual killing there were many involved in the planning of it, and if local tradition is to be believed, six men set out to do the deed.

Robert Louis Stevenson used the incident in his classic story *Kidnapped*, and he made Alan Breck Stewart the murderer. Although

Alan's exploits in *Kidnapped* were pure fiction, Alan himself was a real-life character and one of several men strongly suspected of having done the killing. Shortly after the murder he left the country for France and there wrote a letter admitting his guilt. But many believe that he received a reward for fleeing and allowing the killing to be imputed to him. It was, they believe, all part of a plan to divert suspicion from others.

I doubt if the true identity of the killer will ever be proven, and it is not my intention to try. Instead, I shall simply relate one version of the story which has been passed down in local tradition.

Following the defeat of the Jacobites at Culloden in 1746 the lands and property of those clans which had defied the Hanoverian Government were confiscated by Act of Parliament. Factors were appointed to manage them. The Government chose men who had demonstrated by their actions in the recent conflict that they were strongly anti-Jacobite. Their duties included the granting of leases, the directing of agricultural operations, and the collecting of rents. This last duty was often the most difficult as the clansmen and tenants of the rightful owners of the land would endeavour by every means in their power to withhold the whole or a part of the rents in order to send them to their exiled chiefs.

Colin Campbell of Glenure had been appointed factor on the forfeited estates of Ardshiel, Mamore and Callart. These had formerly been the lands of Cameron of Locheil and the Stewarts of Appin. Campbell had fought in the Hanoverian army and was known for his vicious treatment of those who had supported the Jacobite cause. Two stories illustrate the ruthlessness of this man.

After the Battle of Culloden, the Laird of Kinlochmoidart and the brother of MacDonald of Keppoch were taken prisoner along with a number of common soldiers and in order to avoid being recognised as officers they had removed all marks of distinction. Hanoverian officers examined the prisoners. They recognised Kinlochmoidart and Keppoch and knowing the fate that awaited them should they be discovered, these officers did not let on that they knew them. However, Colin Campbell of Glenure was present. He pointed out the two and they were later brought to trial and found guilty. The sentence carried out upon them was that they were hanged by the neck and taken down before they were dead; their breasts were torn open and their hearts removed and thrown in their faces; their heads were then cut off and their bodies burnt.

Another instance of Campbell's harsh treatment of Jacobites occurred when the relatives of a man killed at Culloden drove away some of the man's cattle to prevent them being taken by the Hanoverian soldiers. Colin Campbell came to hear of it and gave them up to the law. Soldiers were sent to seize them, and though they managed to evade capture they were obliged to flee the country. One of the fugitives, however, did not leave with the others but took refuge at the house of his father-in-law. Campbell was informed that he was there and he went with a party to seize the man. When they arrived at the house it was to the complete surprise of the fugitive. Colin Campbell entered, gun in hand, upon which the young man's mother-in-law put herself between Colin and her son-in-law, thinking that he would not fire at her. 'Oh Colin! Colin! Let him go with his life,' she cried. Colin fired the gun into the woman's breast and killed her. Such deeds as these earned him great hatred among the people and there were many who wished him dead.

Colin Campbell showed no indulgence to the natives of the districts in which he acted as factor, and whenever the opportunity arose he would find reason to evict them. Two of the tenants, acting as a deputation, had a meeting with Campbell to see if they could get him to act more favourably towards them, as many of them were destitute and it was within his power to let them have a living. His reply was, 'I will not stop what I am doing until I leave not a clod of land in the possession of a Stewart in Appin or of a Cameron in Lochaber.'

Campbell was in the habit of walking alone every afternoon near his home. One day the Laird of Callart took a gun and lay in wait at this spot hoping for the opportunity of putting a bullet through him, but on the day he chose, Campbell, on his way to the place where he normally walked, happened to have a chance meeting with a gentleman of his acquaintance with whom he returned to the house and so the opportunity was lost.

Shortly after this some of the principal men in the districts of Appin and Lochaber met to discuss what they ought to do. The organisers of this meeting were obviously in favour of some positive action because they instructed those who had guns to bring them along. Few men were in possession of weapons at the time because the Surrender of Arms Act required them to be handed over to the Government troops. One of the men attending this meeting was named Dugald MacColl. He had a long Spanish gun, and his name for it was the *Slinneanach*. At the meeting all the guns that the men had brought were tested for accuracy, and it was found that the best of them was this gun, the *Slinneanach*. It was capable of putting a bullet and swan-shot within two inches of each other.

It was sensibly agreed that those who had the best guns would give them up to those who were the best shots. A man called Donald Stewart, a nephew of the Laird of Ballachulish, was the best shot among them and MacColl handed over the *Slinneanach* to him. Donald was chosen as one of the men who would attempt to shoot Glenure. The Laird of Fasnacloich was the second-best shot and so he was chosen to accompany Donald. Altogether six men were chosen to lie in ambush, two men in each of three different places.

Colin Campbell of Glenure arranged a visit to Fort William on estate business, and the associates, who were to do the killing, obtained information of the days on which he would be travelling. They decided to ambush him as he was returning to his home in Appin. Big Donald Og MacMartin of Dochanassy and a companion, whose name is not recorded, were to lie in wait at Onich; the Lairds of Callart and Onich were also to be beside the road at Onich but at a distance from the first two; Donald Stewart and the Laird of Fasnacloich were to take up a position between Ballachulish and Lettermore on the southern side of the ferry across Loch Leven which linked Lochaber with Appin to the south.

Colin Campbell left his home in Appin to travel to Fort William on 11 May 1752. On the 14th of the same month Campbell, having completed his business in Fort William, started on his homeward journey. Riding on horseback along with him were his nephew Mungo Campbell and a gillie named Mackenzie. They followed the road that leads along the shores of Loch Linnhe, passed the narrows at Corran, and so on to the small village of Onich. It was here that the first of the six avengers should have been lying in wait. However, Big Donald Og was late in getting to the place, and although his companion had arrived there in good time he had fallen asleep and Glenure's party passed by unmolested. When further along the road the riders came to the second place of ambush the two lairds were ready, hidden on the steeply wooded hillside close to the road. The best shot of the two took aim at Campbell, but Mackenzie the gillie was in the way, riding close beside his master and between the gun and its target. The gillie himself was of the people of Onich, the son of a neighbour, and the Laird was afraid to fire at Colin for fear of hitting Mackenzie.

In the meantime Big Donald Og had arrived at the first place of ambush and he was very angry with his companion for having let the party go unscathed. Leaving his companion behind he ran on along the hillside until he came to the two lairds. Angrily and breathlessly he gasped, 'How have you let the rogue pass without giving him his desert?' After hearing their explanation Donald said, 'Had I been here when he passed I should have fired the shot, although Mackenzie would be killed along with him. I am sure that the able men on the other side will not be so slack as those on this side, and I will not leave this place until I hear the sound of the firing.'

When Colin Campbell and those who were with him reached the ferry they were met there by the one-eyed ferryman Archibald MacInnes whom some believed to be gifted with the Second Sight. It was said that MacInnes could foretell events, but it did not require a man with this gift to know that Colin Campbell had many enemies eagerly awaiting an opportunity to settle accounts. Be it by the gift of Second Sight or by simple deduction, MacInnes saw fit to warn Campbell and advise him not to proceed by his normal route but to take a boat down the middle of the loch and to keep as far from land as possible so that a bullet couldn't reach him. But Campbell told him that although he had been afraid in Lochaber, once across the ferry he would no longer be in fear.

The one-eyed ferryman took the three men and their horses across the water to the Appin side where they remounted and continued their journey. They had not gone far when they met the Laird of Ballachulish who invited them to accept a night's hospitality from him and to continue their journey the following day, but Campbell told him that he was eager to proceed as he had business to settle at Ardshiel. Campbell and Mungo rode on and the Laird of Ballachulish and Mackenzie the gillie followed behind. Campbell and his cousin Mungo rode faster than the two who followed with the result that Ballachulish and the gillie soon lost sight of them.

Donald Stewart and the Laird of Fasnacloich had chosen a spot beside a large black rock. Close to the rock grew an old birch tree with a thick bough growing out from it at a convenient height for them to rest their guns when taking aim. They had made preparations by cutting from the bough any twigs and branches which might obstruct their view; then they carefully loaded and primed their muskets. Donald Stewart had the long Spanish gun the *Slinneanach*, into the barrel of which he had loaded two balls.

When all was ready they sat down to wait in a position from which they could see anyone approaching along the road from Ballachulish, not that they expected to see Colin Campbell because they were confident that one of the four men waiting on the other side of the water would have killed him before he ever reached the ferry. But see him they did. Despite their surprise they kept their heads and coolly and quickly prepared themselves. They waited until Campbell and Mungo drew level with their hiding-place. Donald Stewart, sighting along the barrel of the *Slinneanach*, followed his target and waited until he would have a clear view of Colin Campbell. That moment came after the riders had passed his position and were riding away. He then fired the *Slinneanach*.

The two balls struck Campbell with a dull thud. They entered his left side between his ribs and the armpit. The sound of the shot came a second later and this, combined with the sudden jerk of the rider as the bullets struck, caused his horse to rear and bolt. Campbell cried out, 'Oh Mungo! Mungo! Flee! Flee! I am shot', and he lurched to one side of the horse just as in its headlong dash it reached a gateway in the road. Campbell's weight pulled the horse to one side causing it to narrowly miss hitting the gatepost, but with a sickening sound Campbell himself collided with the post and was thrown heavily into the road.

The Laird of Ballachulish and Mackenzie the gillie heard the shot, and Ballachulish said, "That shot has done harm! I hope that Colin of Glenure is safe.' He then turned his horse and rode back the way he had come, while Mackenzie hurried forward to see how his master fared.

Big Donald Og at Onich also heard the shot and said to the two lairds, 'My business is done now. I may go home. I knew that the gallant men on the other side would not let the rogue pass them in such a silly manner as the men of this side did.'

When Mackenzie arrived at the scene of the shooting he found his master lying dead at the side of the road, his clothing saturated with blood. Mungo told Mackenzie to ride on to the house of James of the Glen and try to get him and others to come and lift Colin of Glenure. After Mackenzie had gone, leaving Mungo kneeling beside the body and attempting to staunch the blood from Colin's wounds, a woman happened along. She was wearing a large handkerchief over her shoulders, and Mungo said to her, 'Were you so good, woman, as to give me your handkerchief I would pay for it.' 'I will not indeed,' said the woman, 'It is in the shop that I bought my handkerchief; go you to the shop and buy a handkerchief as I did.' 'There is a man here,' said Mungo, 'who had been killed by a shot which someone fired at him and it is for quenching the blood that I ask for the handkerchief.' The woman replied, 'Let the hunter now drink the soup,' and she went on her way.

As Mackenzie the gillie approached the house of James of the Glen, James was standing with his back to the fire warming himself, but when Mackenzie knocked at the door, James, not wanting to be seen, hurried into another room. The gillie had seen James through a window. When the wife of James answered the door, the gillie asked if her husband was at home, just as if he had not seen him. The wife, lying, told him that James was not at home. The gillie then told her that his master had been killed between Ballachulish and Lettermore and that he needed men to carry the body. Meanwhile, in the next room, James was hurriedly changing the mud-spattered clothes that he wore for clean and at the same time listening to the conversation taking place in the other room. As soon as he had finished dressing he went through to join his wife and the gillie, and he told Mackenzie that he was willing to go with him. However, his wife was so strongly opposed to it that he quickly changed his mind and told Mackenzie that he would have to find others to do the work.

About a year before this incident James of the Glen, whose proper name was James Stewart, had been evicted by Colin Campbell from his farm in Glen Duror on the estate of Ardshiel. His cattle had been confiscated and his land given to a man of the same clan as Glenure, one Peter Campbell of Breadalbane. After this James Stewart had become much addicted to drink and when he was drunk, as he often was, he would revile Colin of Glenure and threaten that he would do as much harm to Colin as he had done to him. His bitterness was well known. On one occasion when he was drinking in a public house, the health of Colin of Glenure was proposed. James of the Glen said, 'I would not drink the health of Colin of Glenure.' The man who had proposed the toast asked, 'What would you do then?' 'Were he on the gallows I would draw down his feet,' declared James. Someone in the company had taken note of that remark and when, after the killing, a reward was offered to anyone who would give information of those who had ill-will towards Glenure, this person informed the Sheriff of Inveraray of what James had said and he was arrested and sent a prisoner to Fort William.

All those in some way connected with the plot against the life of Colin of Glenure now lived in fear. The relations of Glenure and many gentlemen of the powerful and Government-favoured Clan Campbell were ransacking the country, threatening and accusing. Along with James Stewart, eleven other men had already been arrested on the suspicion of having had something to do with it. Knowing the great danger they were in, those gentlemen involved in the plot now put into operation the plan which they had previously prepared; a plan designed to divert suspicion from themselves. Information was given that Alan Breck Stewart alone had done the killing, and a warrant was immediately issued for his arrest. Prepared for the hue and cry that he knew would follow his being named as the culprit, Alan Breck Stewart had left the district and was keeping himself securely hidden until such time as he could find means of leaving the country and going to France.

While James of the Glen was a prisoner in Fort William he was visited by one of his daughters. Her features very much resembled those of her father, and they were both about the same height. When they were left alone together in the prison cell she suggested to her father that they might exchange clothes so that he could escape, leaving her in his place. But James would not hear of it; to do such a thing would be to put on an appearance of guilt when he was in fact innocent.

On 2 June, James of the Glen was taken from his cell in the Fort to be examined by the Sheriff, George Douglas. His threats against Glenure were given in evidence against him, and he was committed for trial at Inveraray. The trial opened on Thursday, 21 September 1752, before a court composed almost entirely of his enemies and political opponents. On the bench sat the Duke of Argyll, Chief of the hated Clan Campbell and Lord Chief Justice of Scotland, while the jury were Campbells almost to a man.

The evidence produced by the prosecution was of the flimsiest description. The principal witness against James Stewart was a man named John MacColl whom James knew well. MacColl had been left an orphan as a youth. James Stewart had pitied him and given him a home, and he and his wife reared him until he was able to fend for himself, and for many years after James had employed him on his farm. MacColl had been among the company in the public house when James had used harsh words against Colin of Glenure, and he readily gave evidence of every word that he had heard James utter.

MacColl's reasons for wanting to see James condemned are not known, but he appears to have had a personal grudge against him. After giving his evidence MacColl left the court only to return a few minutes later saying he remembered something more that James had said against Glenure, for when MacColl had left the court after giving the first part of his evidence he had met his wife in the street outside, and she had questioned him about the evidence he had given. After hearing him repeat what he had told the court his wife asked him, 'Did you tell them that you heard James of the Glen saying once when he was drunk that he would go a mile on his knees on the ice to make a blackcock of Colin of Glenure?' 'Indeed, I did not remember that,' said John. 'Well,' said his wife, 'you had better return and tell it to them.' 'I do not like to return to the courthouse again since I did not remember it when I was in,' replied John. However, his wife eventually persuaded him to return, and he told the court of what his wife had reminded him.

After a verdict of guilty had been pronounced and James of the Glen condemned to be hanged, Donald Stewart was disposed to give himself up rather than see an innocent man hang for a crime of which he himself was guilty. But when his friends heard of his intention they gathered round him to try to dissuade him. They pointed out to him that Alan Breck Stewart had already feigned that he was the person who killed Colin of Glenure. This had done no good to James of the Glen, and if Donald were to deliver himself up it would only make matters worse, and they might both hang. Although Donald's friends at last convinced him that giving himself up would be futile, Donald himself grew sick with grief and took to his bed where he remained for a long time after.

On the 7 November, James of the Glen was bound to a horse and conducted from Fort William by a guard of one hundred redcoat soldiers to the ferry at Ballachulish. When they reached Ballachulish a storm was blowing and they had to delay their crossing until the following morning. A little after midday they arrived at the place of execution, a hillock known as Cnap a' Chaolais, close to the spot where the crime had been committed. A small tent had been erected beside the gallows and into this the prisoner was led. He was attended by two clergymen, Mr William Caskill, minister of Kilmallie, and Mr Couper, minister of Fort William. After spending a short time in devotion, James produced three copies of a speech he had prepared; one of them he gave to the Sheriff of Argyll, another to Captain Welsh, the commanding officer of the military escort, and he begged leave to read the third. Permission having been granted, he read in a clear and steady voice a speech in which he again strongly affirmed his innocence or any participation in the crime.

'I positively deny,' he said, 'directly or indirectly being accessory to Glenure's murder, nor do I know who was the actor, further than my suspicion of Alan Breck Stewart, founded upon circumstances that have been cast up since the murder happened.' After complaining about the treatment he received while imprisoned at Fort William he went on, 'When my trial came on, I found it was not only Glenure's murder I had to answer for, of which, I thank God, my conscience could easily clear me, but the sins and follies of my forefathers were charged against me, such as the rebellions of 1715, of 1719, and 1745. Thus I have not been allowed the character of an honest man.'

After taking affectionate leave of his friends James mounted the gallows. The storm of the previous night had still not completely abated and so it was amid the howling of the wind and the tears and groans of the assembled people that James Stewart was hanged by the neck until dead. His body was left hanging on the gallows as a warning to others, and as the gallows were within sight of his house, for years thereafter his widow could not look the way of Ballachulish without seeing the grim sight of her husband's decaying remains moving and turning in the wind.

THE ANOINTED MAN

The Anointed Man

As a boy of ten or eleven I would spend my summer holidays from school with a widowed aunt at Eilanmore in the Summer Isles. My aunt was childless, and none of the neighbours had children anywhere near my own age, and so if it had not been for Alasdair I should certainly have been lonely. Alasdair was one of the five sons of Robert Achanna, a crofter and neighbour to my aunt. Alasdair was a friend whom I loved, though he was a man old enough to have been my father. We had much in common, and I never knew anyone more companionable, for all that he was called 'Silent Ally'. Many were the hours I spent talking with Alasdair while he went about his daily tasks on the croft, cutting and carrying the peats or hoeing the turnips, and when Alasdair was at the fishing he would take me along.

Although Alasdair's brothers were younger than he, they were inclined to be morose and they never once showed any friendliness towards me, indeed they showed little enough to their own brother Alasdair. I often heard the contemptuous mockery which not only Alasdair's brothers but even his father used towards him at times. Once, I remember, I was puzzled when on a bleak day in a stormy August I overheard one of his brothers say angrily and scoffingly, 'There goes the Anointed Man!' I looked; but all I could see was that, despite the dreary cold, despite the ruined harvest, despite the rotting potato crop, Alasdair walked slowly onward, smiling and with glad eyes brooding upon the grey lands around and beyond him.

It was nearly a year thereafter – I remember the date because it was that of my last visit to Eilanmore – that I understood more fully. I was walking with Alasdair toward sundown. The light was upon his face as though it came from within; and when I looked again, half in awe, I saw that there was no glamour out of the west, for the evening was dull and threatening rain. Three months before, his brothers Allan and William, had been drowned; a month later, his brother Robert had sickened and now sat in the ingle from morning till the covering of the peats, a skeleton almost, shivering and morosely silent with large, staring eyes. On the large bed in one corner of the room their father old Robert Achanna lay, stricken with paralysis.

As I walked with Alasdair I was conscious of a wellnigh intolerable depression. The house we had left was so mournful. The bleak, sodden pastures were so mournful. So mournful was the stony place we were crossing, silent but for the thin crying of the curlews; and above all so mournful was the sound of the ocean as, unseen, it moved sobbingly round the island – so distressing beyond words was all this to me that I stopped abruptly, meaning to go no further but to return to the house where, at least, there was the warmth of the fire. But when I looked up into my companion's face I saw in truth the light that shone from within. His eyes were upon a forbidding stretch of ground where the blighted potatoes rotted among a wilderness of round skull-white stones. I remember them still; these strange far-blue eyes; lamps of quiet joy; lamps of peace, they seemed to me.

'Are you looking at Achnacarn?' (as the tract was called), I asked in what I am sure was a whisper.

'Yes', replied Alasdair, slowly; 'I am looking. It is beautiful: beautiful. O God, how beautiful is this lovely world!'

I know not what made me act so, but I threw myself on a heathery ridge close by and broke out into convulsive sobbings. Alasdair stooped, lifted me in his strong arms, and soothed me with soft words.

'Tell me, laddie, what is it? What is the trouble?' he asked again and again.

'It is you – it is you, Alasdair,' I managed to say coherently at last. 'It terrifies me to hear you speak as you did a little ago. You must be fey. Why? Why do you call that hateful, hideous field beautiful . . . on this dreary day . . . and after all that has happened? Oh, Alasdair?'

'Is it not beautiful?' he asked plaintively and with tears in his eyes. Then without waiting for my answer, he said quietly, 'Listen, and I will tell you.' He was strangely still – breathless he seemed to me – for a minute or more. Then he spoke:

'I was little more than a child, a boy just like you, when something happened. I was out upon the heather in the time when the honey oozes

in the bells and cups. I had always loved the island and the sea. Perhaps I was foolish, but I was so glad with my joy that golden day that I threw myself on the ground and kissed the hot, swing ling and put my hands and arms into it, sobbing the while with my vague, strange yearning. At last I lay still with my eyes closed. Suddenly I was aware that two tiny hands had come up through the spires of the heather and were pressing something soft and fragrant upon my eyelids. When I opened them, I could see nothing unfamiliar. No one was visible. But I heard a whisper, "Arise and go away from this place at once; and this night do not venture out, lest evil befall you." So I rose, trembling, and went home.

'Thereafter I was the same, and yet not the same. Never could I see, as they saw, what my father and brothers or the islefolk looked upon as ugly or dreary. My father was angry with me many times and called me a fool. Whenever my eyes fell upon those waste and desolate spots, they seemed to me passing fair, radiant with lovely light. At last my father grew so bitter that, mocking me the while, he bade me go to the towns and see there the squalor and sordid hideousness wherein men dwelled. But thus it was with me: in the places they call slums and among the smoke of factories, what I saw was lovely, beautiful with strange glory, and the faces of men and women were sweet and pure. So, weary and bewildered with my unwilling quest, I came back to Eilanmore.

'On the day of my homecoming, Morag was there – Morag of the Falls. She turned to my father and called him blind and foolish. "He has the white light upon his brows," she said of me; "I can see it, like the flicker-light in a wave when the wind's from the south in thunder-weather. He has been touched with the Fairy Ointment. The Guid Folk know him. It will be thus with him till the day of his death. He upon whom the Fairy Ointment has been laid must see all that is ugly and hideous and dreary and bitter through a glamour of beauty. Thus it hath been since the MacAlpin ruled from sea to sea, and thus is it with the man Alasdair, your son."

'That is all, my boy, and that is why my brothers, when they are angry, sometimes call me the Anointed Man.'

Oh, Alasdair Achanna! How often have I thought of that most precious treasure you found in the heather. Which of us would not barter the best of all our possessions – and some there are who would surrender all – to have one touch laid upon the eyelids – one touch of the Fairy Ointment?

Adapted from a story by Fiona Macleod, 'Under the Dark Star', 1899.

THE BLACK CAPTAIN

The Black Captain

When the suffix Dubh is applied by Highlanders to an individual it is most often because that person has black hair, but in some cases the word Dubh refers to the character rather than to the physical appearance. For instance, Am Fear Dubh and Domhnull Dubh are terms frequently applied to the Devil.

Captain Macpherson of the Black Watch or 42nd Highlanders was known in his native glen by the cognomen of An-t-Offigeach Dubh (the Black Officer). Whether this was because of his raven-black hair, or because he was an officer in the Black Watch, or because of his evil character I do not know; but this I do know, that if we take into consideration the many disreputable methods he adopted for pressing his fellow countrymen into the then broken ranks of the 42nd Highlanders, a more appropriate name he could not possibly have been given. It was even said that he had sold himself to Satan. We need not, therefore, wonder that he was more feared than loved in his native district.

Captain Macpherson resided at Ballachroan House, midway between Kingussie and Newtonmore. This ancient building is pleasantly situated in a clump of evergreen and other trees on the northern slopes of the Valley of the Spey. It is built in the old Baronial style of granite and whinstone; it is two storeys high and slated with grey stones taken from a neighbouring quarry. It is said to be the oldest inhabited house in the district.

Some of the terms of agreement which existed between the Captain and the Devil are handed down to us. The Evil One promised to give him whatever he might desire for a specified period with a few trifling reservations. The Captain's first request was that the crops planted in the lands of Ballachroan should for their extraordinary fruitfulness be a wonder to all who saw or heard of them. To this the Devil agreed, provided he would get the roots. That year the Captain put down a grain crop only, and for quality and fertility the like of it was never seen in Badenoch. He reaped his fields in the usual way and when the Devil came for his share of the crop the Captain coolly told him to take the roots according to their agreement. Satan complained of this treatment and insisted that he had been cheated. 'Well, then,' said the Captain, 'I'll give you the crop next year and I'll take the roots myself.' And to this the Devil readily agreed.

The following year the Captain planted a root crop – potatoes, turnips, carrots, etc. – which turned out the best and most productive ever seen in the country. At the proper time he began to lift his crop, but scarcely had he begun when Satan appeared on the scene and demanded his share. The Captain mockingly pointed to the 'shaws' and said, 'There it is. Take it.' Satan fumed with rage and told the Captain that he would not cheat him a third time.

The Captain next asked for a crop of cattle, which for quality, beauty and fruitfulness was never excelled. The Devil agreed to this on condition that all the animals nearest the corner of the steading should be his share. The Captain immediately set to work, pulled down his farm steading and built a circular one in its place, and he had a crop of cattle the following year which far exceeded anything ever heard of. Satan called for his share of the cattle at the proper time and was told to take all he could claim. On looking at the steading and finding that there were no corners in it he positively screamed with rage.

The Captain's *modus operandi* to secure recruits for the 42nd was to attend every market, ball and gathering in the district and there mingle freely with all the beau-ideals present, to whom he would give whisky in unmeasured quantities, and when they became wholly insensible, he would, in the King's name, press a shilling into each man's hand. If, however, anyone present were wary enough, as not infrequently happened, to decline more mountain dew than was good for him, the Captain would put a shilling into his glass or slip one unawares into his pocket, and then with stern and fearful imprecations declare that his man was now enlisted and thus compelled to leave all that was near and dear to him in this world.

It was no uncommon thing for him sometimes to follow a young man slyly on the road and slip a shilling unobserved into his pocket; or, if meeting one going in the opposite direction, he would throw a shilling towards the man and, if he caught it, he would find himself sent off to the wars. Many a fond mother, loving sister and other loved ones in the districts of Badenoch, Strathspey and Strathdearn, heaped their blackest curses upon his head for these cruel acts, invoked heaven's direst vengeance to fall upon him and secretly prayed that the Devil himself would take him away from their midst to the place of torment.

On one occasion, going to church in his native strath on a pleasant Sunday afternoon, the Captain found himself within a few hundred yards of the place of worship walking immediately behind the reverend gentleman who was to preach that day. He was a young man of prepossessing appearance, and in the handsome black suit in which he was attired was the very model of a real Highlander – five feet ten inches in height, proportionably stout, erect in stature, having well-defined limbs and square shoulders above which was a finely shaped head with glossy dark and curly hair. 'You are too fine a figure,' muttered the Captain to himself as he gazed at the minister, 'to be dressed in black clothes. A red coat would set you off to greater advantage, and I shall be much disappointed unless you have a red one on your back before long.'

The Captain went to church but derived little benefit from the earnest and impressive discourse delivered by the young preacher, for his mind was wholly absorbed with a different theme – how he could enlist the minister for a soldier – and every time the preacher turned his massive chest in the direction of the Captain his dermination to enlist him at whatever cost increased.

The minister was the only son of a poor widow who lived in an obscure corner of the strath and by ten o'clock the following Monday morning the Black Captain was seen standing at the door waiting for admission. He had hardly seated himself when he made known his errand, a circumstance which, as might be expected, threw the poor widow into a paroxysm of fear. On recovering somewhat, she appealed to the Captain to have some compassion on the tender feelings of a devoted mother and poor widow and abandon his intention of taking her beloved and only son from her side; that if he persisted in his cruel design he would send her broken-hearted to the grave long before her time. The only response from the Captain to her entreaties was, 'It is a pity and a shame to see such a good-looking young man dressed in black clothes.' Without any further preliminaries he threw a shilling into the minister's bosom, and left. The young minister was soon marched off to Edinburgh where the depot of the 42nd Highlanders was then stationed.

The Black Captain saw a good deal of active service in his day. He took part in several severe engagements in the West Indies where he greatly distinguished himself, demonstrating to all that he was a warrior of no mean order. Having retired from the army with a captain's pension, he resided almost continuously afterwards with his wife and family at Ballachroan House and spent his time at the chase, a sport to which he was devotedly attached. Although there were little or no restrictions on deer forests in Badenoch and Strathspey in those days, they were all free to the Black Captain.

His special and favourite place of resort was the Forest of Gaick and more than once did he remain overnight in a shieling hut. This was a strong structure of its kind. Its walls were built of stone and sods, and for greater stability its couples were driven deep into the ground below the foundations of its walls. The valley, which is upwards of twelve miles from Kingussie, is surrounded by wild and rugged mountains, and the shieling, facing the north-west, stood on a somewhat elevated spot at the base of the mountains on the east side of the valley.

On the morning of 25 December 1799 the Captain, accompanied by six stalwart Highlanders, started for the Forest of Gaick. They took provisions along with them sufficient to last three days, intending to lodge as usual in the shieling, into which a quantity of peats and moss fir had previously been stored to be ready for use when required. The weather was all that a sportsman could desire – clam, bright and frosty. The hunters' success that day was rather indifferent, but that was of little consequence as they could have any amount of venison on the morrow.

Entering the shieling in the evening they lit a fire and on the red embers broiled a portion of their newly killed venison. After doing ample justice to an excellent repast, they sat round a brilliant fire cheerfully burning before them, reciting stories, singing songs and emptying their cups of mountain dew. The night thus wore on unperceived, and the hilarity was increasing when a loud knock was heard at the door which startled every one in the shieling. Terror seized the bravest man; yea, even the Black Captain himself looked aghast and stared wildly around. 'That was not the knock of an earthly being – no human creature could be there tonight – what on earth could it be?' were thoughts that passed with lightning speed through their minds. But scarcely were their thoughts conceived when the knock was repeated, and louder than before – so loud that the sound apparently shook the shieling.

The Captain immediately started up, and as his companions looked at each other in blank amazement and quaked with fear, proceeded to the door, which he boldly opened and, stepping outside, closed the door behind him. Seeing this, one of his companions Alex Macpherson, more courageous than his fellows, crept softly up to the door, and peeping through the chink in the wood, was horrified to observe a large he-goat with huge horns and keen restless eyes sparkling fierce and bright like those of the rattlesnake. It was in deep conversation with the Captain.

As they spoke in an inaudible tone, Macpherson, though quite close to them, heard but little of what passed between them, but that little was enough to make the stoutest heart quail, for he heard enough to satisfy him that their nocturnal visitor was none other than the Prince of the Lower Regions, who had that night in terms of a previous agreement come in person for the Black Captain. He gathered further from their conversation that the Captain denied that this was the night on which he had agreed to give himself up; that it was that night week. The he-goat agreed to postpone the fulfilment of the original compact for a week from that night, providing that the Captain would have five men in addition to himself in readiness to join them in the Valley of Gaick; also that the Captain agreed to these stipulations.

Macpherson began now to tremble so violently that he was unable to hear anything further that passed between them. As he was in great danger of being discovered by them, he crawled back to his companions who were, like himself, almost prostrate with terror. On reaching the fire, he communicated the fearful intelligence while they looked at each other in blank amazement and trembled in every limb.

Macpherson had hardly done speaking when the Captain joined them, exhibiting an unusually gloomy and sullen aspect. Some terrible thoughts seemed to occupy his mind during the remainder of the night. None of them went to rest. The heather shakedowns which were arranged along the wall opposite the fire were left unoccupied, and although the Captain tried hard to keep up a conversation and look cheerful, he singularly failed; and it was only after he had emptied several cups that he mastered proper command of his usual composure and natural ease. Few words were exchanged between him and his companions during the rest of the night.

They were early astir next morning. Having been more than usually successful at the chase this day, they left the forest early in the evening with heavy burdens of venison. Reaching their respective homes shortly after nightfall, they thanked Providence for bringing them safe out of the forest and vowed that they would never again accompany the Black Captain to the same place.

The report spread rapidly through the whole of Badenoch that Satan had at last come for the Black Captain, and that it was arranged between them to meet in the Forest of Gaick precisely a week from the date of their last meeting. This report, especially that part of it which referred to the Captain promising him five men along with himself, threw the district into the greatest alarm, and this profound excitement grew more intense as the end of the week of grace approached.

The men who formed the Captain's hunting expedition on the last occasion were those who generally accompanied him to the chase in the past, and fearing that he might compel them to go with him again to Gaick, some of them left the country, while others hid in caves and caverns or in their houses.

A day or two prior to the night on which the Captain promised to meet the he-goat, he called upon his gillies for the purpose, as he alleged, of accompanying him to the forest to procure a supply of venison for the Christmas feast, which was then observed in Badenoch in the good old style; but with the exception of Alex Macpherson, he found that they had all disappeared. This circumstance infuriated him so much that, in order to discover them or be avenged if he failed to find them, he set fire to some of their houses and pulled others down, for he well knew that they disappeared from fear of the consequences expected when he again met Domhnull Dubh. He found none of them.

Having no time to lose, he immediately went to Strathdearn, where he easily procured four fox-hunters who promised to accompany him to the chase in Gaick Forest. These, with Macpherson, the Badenoch man, made up the necessary number. It was considered remarkable that Macpherson, knowing as he did so much of what had passed between the he-goat and the Captain on the night of 25 December, offered no objection to go there again. Such was the case; but he was the only one of the hunters who did not avow that he would not go. The evening before they were to start, Macpherson's wife was indefatigable in her endeavours to get her husband persuaded from going. She pressed him so hard that he exclaimed, 'Surely you do not know the Black Captain's nature when you would urge me to act thus. Let me tell you that if I refuse to go along with him he will shoot me like a dog the next time he sees me.'

The men were to meet the Captain on the appointed day at a point on the south side of the River Spey, nearly opposite Ballachroan House. When Macpherson was leaving his house for the place of rendezvous, he was attacked by his own dogs, forcing him back through the door. His wife then advised him as he valued his life to remain at home; that Providence had put it into the hearts of the dogs to keep him from going and that if he still refused this warning, the consequences would be alarming. He yielded at last to her importunities and said, 'Where can I go and conceal myself that he will not find me?' 'Leave that with me,' she answered, and immediately placed him in an all-but-forgotten cavity in an out-of-the-way corner of his home.

It was on the morning of 31 December 1799 when the Black Captain met the Strathdearn hunters at the place of rendezvous on the south side of the Spey. Having waited some time for Macpherson, and seeing that he did not join them as promised, the Captain went to his house to see what had detained him. Finding that he, too, had disappeared he became furious, swore dire vengeance against Macpherson and his wife, and set off at once to join the Strathdearn men. They started forthwith for the Forest of Gaick.

It had been freezing keenly for several days and now it was clear and frosty. The Captain was dressed in a singularly strange garb – a pair of coarse homespun, undyed, plaiding breeches, vest, coat, and plaid, and on his head a black fur bonnet; his stockings were of grey wool; his shoes, made by himself, of untanned hide. To give some idea of the severity of the frost at that time, it may be mentioned that the Captain crossed the Spey on the ice opposite his own house. The party took sufficient food with them for three days.

In consequence of the delay caused by the various disappointments before setting out on their journey, the day was far advanced before they reached their destination; but whether they went to the hunt that evening or waited till the dawn of the next day it is impossible to say for the last that was seen of them alive was ascending the hills above Nuide Beag, then a flourishing hamlet, in the direction of the forest.

On that night – 31 December – the heavens were calm and cloudless, but a terrific storm suddenly burst forth and swept over the mountain-tops with great fury. The flashes of lightning were so vivid and in such rapid succession that the sky over Gaick seemed all ablaze, while the thunder peals were so loud and terrible that the stoutest heart in Badenoch quaked with terror. And although this storm swept over the whole of Scotland, its raging fury seemed to be concentrated in the Forest of Gaick, where its awful magnitude was beyond all power of description.

This unparalleled tempest of wind, snow, thunder and lightning ceased with the break of the following morning, but the wind and drifting snow continued without any abatement during the next two days and nights, when it died away almost into a dead calm. The dreadful storm that prevailed, combined with the no less dreadful personage who was to meet the Black Captain in Gaick the very night on which the storm began, excited a universal belief in Badenoch that the hunters and their Captain had perished.

As soon, therefore, as the weather permitted, a party consisting of twelve brave men set out to the forest to look for the Captain and his companions, and on reaching the valley, which presented a melancholy and dreary waste, they were horrified to find that the shieling had entirely disappeared. As they proceeded from the lower end of the valley towards the place where it stood, they came upon some stones which formed part of the walls, pieces of wood, and the divots which formed the roof cropping up here and there among the snow at a distance of two to three hundred yards from the site of the shieling. The lintel of the door, which was a heavy block of granite, lay at least a hundred yards distant, and on account of the immense depth of snow on the ground (at least six feet) it was only discovered after the most diligent and persevering search. All that was left intact of the once-strong shieling was a small portion of the back wall which was below the level of the surrounding earth.

The bodies of four of the unfortunate sufferers were found dreadfully mangled – some say they were torn limb from limb – in different parts of the valley. The body of the other unfortunate man was found some three months afterwards, two or three hundred yards from where the shieling had stood.

When the snow cleared away from the valley the very heather, for a considerable distance all around the site, was found to be uprooted clean out of the earth. Many pieces of mountain rock were torn away by the storm and lay strewn through the valley. The dogs were not only killed but their bones were broken in pieces. Some of the guns were found and these were broken and bent, twisted like corkscrews.

There is one other anecdote in connection with this remarkable affair. It is positively affirmed that when the bodies were being removed from Gaick it was utterly impossible to remove the Black Captain's from the spot until it was first turned face downwards, and that when the procession was formed the body was, out of respect for his rank, placed at the head. But one mishap after another occurred in such rapid succession to those who carried it that it was found impossible to make any progress on the journey. Observing this, a sage who was present said, 'Place the fellow in the rear, and I venture to promise that you will meet with no further hindrance till you reach home.' Effect was immediately given to this suggestion and the procession proceeded without further interruption to Kingussie.

Considering all these circumstances, we need hardly wonder that the whole episode was ascribed to supernatural agency. The storm, the destruction of the shieling, and some of the other terrible events connected with this catastrophe are recorded in the muse of a Celtic bard who flourished at the time.

The Black Captain's remains were interred near the west end of the burying-ground which is now known as 'Cladh a Mhuillinn Chardaidh' and situated at the west end of the village of Kingussie. The conclusion of the inscription on his gravestone is as follows: 'Died 2nd January 1800, aged 62 years.' How it could be ascertained that he died on 2 January was then and still is a matter of much controversy in the district. The general belief is that he and his companions were killed during the first night of the tempest – the morning of 1 January 1800.

Adapted and abridged from a story published in *The Celtic Magazine*, 1878.

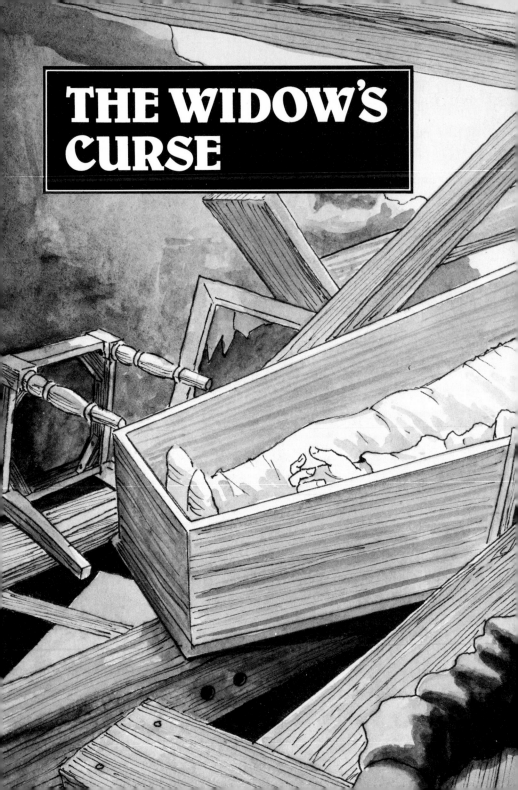

The Widow's Curse

Glenfalcon is one of the most charming places in the Highlands. The beautiful bay which bears its name is in the form of a horseshoe, round which the little village is built. On three sides the bay is surrounded by hills and walls of rock sloping towards the sea. Outside the bay, to the east, lies a picturesque loch – a long, narrow inlet of the sea with two pretty islands at its mouth. To the north is a narrow stretch of fertile land, while the Isle of Skye lies to the west, thus forming a great basin of water sheltered on every side. In the centre of this basin lies a beautiful group of islands making as fair a scene as the eye could wish to rest upon.

On the western side of the bay is a fine glen, divided into two parts by the action of a mountain torrent, that by long ages of hard work has made a deep bed for itself in the solid rock through which it tumbles noisily till it reaches the bay. In this glen the mournful spectacle of seven or eight ruined cottages may still be seen. These humble dwellings were desolated and their inhabitants turned adrift to find other homes or starve by the despotic will of one man.

Our story opens on a beautiful evening in the middle of August some time last century. The sun is just disappearing over the cliffs and its parting rays throw a red glow over the sails of the fishing-boats in the bay. A few old women, too feeble to do harder work, sit at their doors spinning or knitting. Among them is a widow named Cameron and her daughter, Jessie, a delicate child of twelve years, who is employed in reading aloud. Mrs Cameron's husband was drowned at the herring-fishing two years before, and the widow and her child had been left totally unprovided for. The men of the West are under the necessity of risking their lives at the fishing as, in consequence of the unjust laws, they cannot get a living from the soil.

The neighbours were willing to assist the poor widow to the full extent of their power; but as one cannot get blood from a stone, neither can money be got from people who are drained of their last farthing by the exactions of rack-renting landlords. The kindly people did what they could to help the widow and the fatherless child by tilling her little croft for her. Thus, with a struggle, Mrs Cameron managed to live and keep Jessie at school. The poor child had always been delicate; the cold breath of winter in that northern isle dealt hardly with her. During the two previous winters she had suffered much and she was yet very weak and ailing, sorely needing that good living and medical advice which her mother's poverty prevented her from having. She was like a summer flower that could only live in the bright sunshine. The widow dreaded the approach of winter on the account of the suffering it caused to her only child, whom she loved more than her own life.

Owing to an exceptionally bad season, the crofters had been unable to pay their rents at the last term. The proprietor of the estate was a hard, stern man. No excuses would be accepted by him for non-payment of rent. When informed that his tenants were unable to pay and craved a little indulgence until the next summer, he gave orders to his factor that unless he were paid, not only the sum due at Martinmas but also the arrears, the tenants, one and all, should be evicted.

These harsh instructions were duly made known to the people; but what could they do? They had no money and they had no place to go. The next year's rent was due on 11 November so, after consulting together, they drew up an urgent appeal for indulgence till the summer. The only reply vouchsafed was a repetition of the former threat. The people were in despair but were powerless to help themselves; their only hope was that at the last moment the landlord might relent. In this miserable state of uncertainty the dreaded 11 November came and passed without any further communication between the landlord and his tenants.

On the morning of 23 November, the head factor of the estate, the under-factor, a sheriff-officer and a party of policemen made their way to Glenfalcon. This was the landlord's answer to the tenants' appeal for mercy. It was a bitterly cold morning; the snow was falling heavily, and the piercing north wind was enough to freeze the marrow in one's bones. Everything looked dreary and miserable. It was bad enough to be obliged to live in such wretched hovels as the poor people had at any time, even in the middle of summer; but this armed party came to turn the inhabitants out into the bleak winter day, leaving them no shelter but the snow-laden sky, and no flooring but the snow-covered heath.

In the first house the evicting party entered there lived a man named Macdonald who was out at the time, but his wife and his seven children, clad only in rags, half famished and crouching round a mere handful of peat fire, was a sight that might have moved even the hardest of hearts. On seeing such a formidable party enter her poor dwelling, the poor woman started to her feet and cried out in alarm, 'Oh! What are you going to do?'

'Don't you know,' replied Macneil, the under-factor, 'That we have orders to turn you out?'

'But surely,' pleaded the poor woman, 'you will not turn us out in this weather – in the snow. What will become of my poor children?'

'You were warned, and you must go,' replied Macneil gruffly, trying to hide his feelings of pity under a rough exterior. 'It is not my fault. Blame your landlord, Mr Campbell, not me. I must obey orders.'

He, anxious to shift all responsibility for such cruelty from his own shoulders, spoke to the factor and asked if they were to proceed with the disagreeable task. The answer was a peremptory order to remove the furniture at once. At this moment the husband, Macdonald, returned and took in the situation at a glance; but he was perfectly helpless in the matter and could only look on with an apathy born of despair, while his few poor household goods were roughly thrown outside. He and his family were then ordered to leave the house and the roof was quickly pulled down, the door was fastened with lock and key, and the wretched family were forbidden even to seek the shelter afforded by the four bare walls of their late home.

Who can tell the agony that wrings a father's and a mother's heart in a case like this? Their house ruined, their children starving with hunger, and cold, no place to go for shelter, not a gleam of hope anywhere. No wonder that they should pray that death would soon end their unbearable misery.

Regardless of the tears of mothers and children and the earnest expostulations of wellnigh desperate men, the evicting party proceeded from house to house, leaving behind them untold misery and desolation. At length they came to the humble house of Mrs Cameron, which was the last habitation in the glen. The widow fell on her knees and clasped her hands imploringly.

'Have mercy; have mercy,' she cried, 'my child is dying. If you turn us out in this bitter weather, it will kill her at once. Surely you would not commit murder?'

'My good woman,' replied the factor, affected in spite of himself at the scenes of heart-breaking misery he had caused, 'It is useless asking me for mercy. I cannot help myself. Your daughter may be very ill, but my orders are imperative and I must obey.'

He then walked away and left his subordinate to carry out the distasteful orders. Macneil entered the little room where Jessie lay in bed, with death legibly written in her wasted form and attenuated features.

She cried, 'Oh, Mr Macneil, you will not turn us out. Look, it is snowing,' pointing to the little window. 'We will die in the snow; you will not be so cruel.'

Macneil turned aside to hide the feelings which he was ashamed to show, but which did credit to his manhood.

'If,' he muttered, 'I dared feel for anyone, it would be for this poor child and her widowed mother; but I cannot afford to pity anyone.'

Then turning again to the sick girl he said, 'Indeed, it is not my fault, Jessie, that you must go; but if I can find a place of shelter anywhere, I will.'

He then went out and left the rest of the party to do their dirty work. Their little furniture was soon thrown out, and the heart-broken mother, lifting her dying child in her arms, tottered out into the snow crying aloud in her misery, 'Heaven pity us, for man will not; there is nothing left for us but to die.'

'Hush, mother,' said Jessie, 'do not talk so. Mr Macneil says he will try to find us shelter somewhere.'

Soon the work of destruction was completed. The roof was torn off and the snow was falling on the hearth, where the remains of the peat fire still smouldered. The men had buttoned their coats and were preparing to depart, when they were startled by a dreadful scream from Mrs Cameron who fell fainting to the ground, and no wonder, for her beloved Jessie had just expired. She died as many others have died in the Highlands of Scotland and in the south and west of Ireland, a victim to the unjust land laws of our country – laws which deliver arbitrary power into the hands of one class, which is only too often used to crush and oppress another. But these victims have not suffered in vain; their blood has cried aloud for justice, and we are at length awakening to the full knowledge of the cruelties perpetrated under the shadow of these iniquitous laws, the repeal of which the nation now demands with a voice of thunder not to be ignored.

When the widow recovered consciousness, her first words were, 'My daughter!' She staggered to her feet, and clasping the dead body of her child in her arms, covered her cold face with passionate kisses; then with a lingering hope she eagerly placed her trembling hand on her child's heart, only to find that it was indeed still for ever. She looked once more on the calm, white face on which the snow was thickly falling; she looked at her ruined home, and then again at her dead child, when a heart-rending cry of bitter anguish broke from her pallid lips, the cry of a broken heart, from which all joy and hope had now been forever crushed.

With her grey locks falling in disorder over her pale face and her eyes fiercely gleaming with a strange light, she turned to the group of awestruck men and, pointing to the corpse, cried, 'You have murdered her; I call God to witness that you have murdered her. But you are not so much to blame as your master. Listen! Here, in the sight of heaven and by the side of my ruined home and my dead child, I curse him and pray that if there is justice in heaven it will fall and crush him as he has crushed others.'

As the poor woman uttered these fearful words she raised her clenched hands and streaming eyes to heaven. She spoke sensibly enough, but alas, the bystanders saw only too well by her excited gestures and that lurid light that shot from her eyes that the light of reason had fled, and that she was mad.

'I think,' said the factor, 'we had better take her with us. She is certainly out of her mind.'

'I think we had,' agreed Macneil, 'and let us go at once. No good can come of this day's work.'

So, taking the widow and the body of her daughter along with them, they turned down the glen. It would be difficult to picture a more heart-rending scene than that which they had to pass through on their way out of the place. Every hut was destroyed, and the poor wretches who had been so ruthlessly evicted crouched under the walls of their ruined homes for shelter from the ever-increasing storm. Old men and women who could scarcely walk; little children who did not understand what was happening, and sick people who had to be carried out sat there shivering and moaning with cold and grief. More than one of the poor wretches died soon afterwards from the effects of the exposure.

Hastening to quit such a painful scene, the men hurried forward and soon reached the mouth of the glen, where the road runs along the brow of a steep cliff overhanging the torrent rushing and foaming below.

When they had reached this point, the widow, who had hitherto accompanied them quite quietly, suddenly broke away and with a wild cry rushed forward and, before they could prevent her, flung herself over the cliff. A moment later all that remained of the hapless woman was a mangled mass of quivering flesh lying on the rocks below.

Mr Campbell's house stood in a little wood close to the sea. The mountain stream that came tumbling down the rocks ran almost past his door ere it lost itself in the waters of the bay. About two hundred yards from the house the stream was spanned by a wooden bridge, and close beside this bridge was situated the little graveyard of Glenfalcon. Here they buried the poor widow and her child, beside some others who had died from the effects of the harsh proceedings which had been so ruthlessly carried out a few days previously. The news of the tragic results from the recent evictions had spread all over the district; consequently, large numbers gathered to the funerals of the victims of the oppression.

A single glance at the gloomy faces of the bystanders revealed the fact that there were other feelings at work besides the usual grief at the death of relations and neighbours, and after the interment was over and as the people wended their way home in groups, many were the comments made on the widow's sad fate and on her curse. A new feeling animated the people. Men asked themselves why such things should be allowed; yea, and have the sanction of the law, too. And the first dawning of the spirit of independence and determination for justice which will never again be stilled until the present land laws are abolished, began that day to stir in the breasts of the long-suffering people. Men would once more dare to call their souls their own, without fear of laird or factor.

The day of the funeral was excessively gloomy. The sky was heavy with unshed rain. A thaw had set in and the ground was like a sponge. That night the rain fell in torrents, and it continued to fall unabated the whole of the next day and night. Not for many years had the inhabitants seen anything approaching the violence of the present storm. All nature seemed to be weeping; inky clouds obscured the sun, so that it appeared more like night than day. As night came on the storm grew still worse; the people cowered in their miserable huts, listening with awestricken faces and sinking hearts to the pelting rain, the roar of the mountain torrent, and the loud blast of the wind, which threatened every moment to blow their frail dwellings into space.

On this dreary night Mr Campbell sat alone in the parlour of his house. A tall, spare man with a cold, hard face, indicative of a stern unyielding nature. No affectionate wife smoothed the wrinkles from his brow; no loving children climbed on his knee and taught the stern mouth to smile; for he was a bachelor, wrapped up in his own selfishness.

The unusual severity of the storm even disturbed the nerves of this iron-willed man. He could not settle to his reading; his thoughts oppressed him and, as he walked restlessly through the room, he muttered, 'I do not know what is the matter with me tonight. A feeling of dread which I cannot shake off hangs about me. I wish Macneil had not given me such full particulars of that affair up the glen the other day. The woman cursed me, too. Tuts! I am getting superstitious, when the ravings of a mad woman could thus affect me.'

A louder blast than ever, that threatened to break in the window, made him start and look shudderingly round the room as if he half expected to see the ghost of the widow by his side. Rousing himself with an effort from the eerie feeling creeping over him, he went to the window and, drawing up the blind, looked out, but he could see nothing but the big raindrops running down the glass; all without was dense darkness. Turning away with a muttered oath, he sat down before the fire and stirred it into a ruddy glow; the next moment he again started to his feet, as his eyes fell on a picture of The Deluge which hung over the mantelpiece.

'I cannot bear to look on that picture tonight; it makes me feel more miserable than ever,' he said. 'I wish the night was over; I can hear the torrent roaring as if it meant to sweep the house away. I never felt so nervous before; I must have something to cheer me up.'

Ringing the bell, he ordered the servant to bring some whisky and hot water, and then she might retire for the night, as he should want nothing more. Determined to shake off his most unusual depression of spirits, he mixed a stiff glass of toddy, and sitting down to the table busied himself with his accounts. Finding the whisky cheered him up, he did not spare it but continued drinking and writing until near midnight, when suddenly he dropped his pen and started up with fright. The tempest seemed to have reached a climax; the howling of the wind and the roar of the stream now mingled with an appalling sound of rushing water.

'Good heavens! What was that?' he cried in alarm. 'I thought I heard a rush of water close by, but there is such a terrible noise outside that I can hardly distinguish one sound from another; perhaps it was only the wind, or my excited imagination.' Thus saying, he again resumed his seat and mixed another toddy.

Before long his deep potations began to tell. His pen dropped from his fingers, his head sank on his breast, and he fell into a profound sleep. In a little while his heavy breathing and convulsive movements showed that his sleep was anything but refreshing. Suddenly he woke with a start and cried out in a terror-stricken voice, 'Keep off! Go back to the grave! Go back to the grave!'

In his agitation he overthrew the table and upset the lamp, which became extinguished, thus leaving the room in darkness. This increased his fright, and he rushed wildly to the door only to find it locked. He had locked it to secure himself from intrusion and had placed the key on the table and now in the pitch darkness was unable to find it. He was now thoroughly awake but trembling in every limb from the effects of his frightful dreams. His horror of the supernatural was changed into a vivid fear for his personal safety, as he discovered what he had not in his agitation noticed before – that he was standing ankle deep in water.

He shouted in vain for assistance; his voice was drowned in the fearful noise of the hurricane. Nearly at his wit's end he ran to the window; it was firmly fastened, and his agitation was too great to allow him to open it. Every moment the water was rising; now it was up to his knees, and the furniture began to float about. In utter desperation he smashed the glass of the window, but the heavy frame defied his utmost endeavours. All the while the water kept rising steadily, inch by inch. In vain the unhappy man threw himself against the door and then tried to force out the window, only to cut and bruise himself.

He at length realised that he was doomed; the water had now reached his waist, and as he now recalled the window's curse, he cried aloud in his agony at its speedy fulfilment, as he found himself entombed alive with no companion but the merciless water, ever creeping up higher and higher. He climbed upon some furniture and was clinging despairingly to a shelf, when with a loud crash the door was broken from without. The volume of water that rushed in bore a black object which, striking Mr Campbell on the side, threw him backward and knocked him senseless on to the floor. There he speedily drowned.

On this memorable night Macneil, the factor, went to the house of a tenant on the other side of the bay to transact some business. He stayed until a late hour hoping the storm would abate, but at last, seeing no hope of its getting better, he determined to face it. So wishing his neighbour goodnight, he put on his greatcoat and, lantern in hand, set out on his way home. He had nearly two miles to go, but as he knew every inch of the road, he had no fear of losing his way though the darkness was such as might be felt.

'I did not think it was quite so bad as this,' he said to himself, as he groped his way half-blinded by the rain which beat in his face, 'but I won't turn back now I have started; I will go home, be the weather ever so bad.'

Slowly and cautiously he plodded on until he reached the hollow where the bridge spanned the stream. Here he was up to his knees in water and, as he stood for a moment to gain breath, he could hear the torrent as it thundered down the rocks with terrific force, and he said, 'I should not be surprised to find the bridge damaged; I must be careful.' So, holding his lantern before him, he slowly and cautiously advanced. He knew he must be near the bridge, and once over that he would be safe, as the road was uphill and his home was within three hundred yards of it. Just then his progress was arrested by something that lay like a log of wood right across his path; lowering his lantern, he peered through the darkness to see what it was. His horror can be imagined when he saw that it was a coffin, the lid of which had been partly torn off, and the ghastly face of a dead man met his horrified gaze. Firm as were Macneil's nerves, they received a rude shock, but a moment's thought was sufficient for him to regain his self-possession. He rightly conjectured that the torrent had overflowed and had washed part of the graveyard away, and he was more than every convinced of the necessity of the greatest caution on his part as doubtless the bridge had likewise been destroyed.

Suddenly, so suddenly that he never clearly comprehended how it happened, he felt himself lifted off the ground and carried away on a swift stream of rushing water. He was a powerful swimmer but swimming was of little avail in such a mad torrent, especially encumbered as he was with heavy clothes. He struggled desperately to keep above water, but he must have gone down had he not managed to catch hold of a piece of wood as it floated past him. Clinging to this he was borne swiftly along until, at last, he was dashed against what appeared to be a wall. The top was about two feet above the level of the water, and though greatly exhausted and severely bruised by his rapid transit through the flood, Macneil managed to climb to the top of this wall.

He had now time to rest and collect his scattered senses as he lay on the wall and held on with both hands. The storm still raged with great fury; all around him was a mass of rushing, seething water, but he could distinguish the sound of the wind among trees and he at once knew he must be near the proprietor's house, as there were no trees anywhere else in this direction. a terrible thought crossed his perturbed mind. What if Mr Campbell's house had been swept away, and the inmates drowned? He might be even now on one of the ruined walls for all he knew. The more he considered, the more convinced he became that it must be so. The house occupied a very low position, to which the water would inevitably rush, after sweeping away the bridge; and he thought, if he were indeed on the ruins of Mr Campbell's house, he might be able to get a safer and more comfortable position than the one he now occupied.

He very slowly and carefully crawled along the top of the wall until he came to an angle where the wall rose higher. This was what he expected, and he still continued to grope his way along, feeling on the inner side of the wall with his hands to ascertain if any part of the rooms remained intact. At last he felt what were evidently some slates, which he knew must have fallen on the floor of one of the upper rooms. He cautiously lowered himself, still keeping a firm hold on the wall with both his hands, until he tested the strength of the standing place. Finding it firm, he did not venture further but sat down on the floor under the slight shelter afforded by the fragment of wall left standing.

Fortunately, he had some matches in a tin box in an inner pocket which the water had not reached, so striking one he attempted to ascertain his position. He saw that he was in the ruins of a room in the upper storey; nearly all the roof had fallen, and the floor on which he stood was covered with the debris. A few feet from where he stood was a great hole in the floor through which he would have fallen had he ventured to move forward without a light. Although his situation was bad enough, he felt in comparative safety, especially as the gale was lessening in force and the water evidently subsiding, so he made up his mind to stay where he was until morning when he could see where to go.

Body and mind had now been on the rack for at least five hours. The sense of safety took away the excitement that had acted like a stimulant while he was in danger, and although drenched to the skin and very imperfectly sheltered from the storm, he fell asleep. But, as may be readily imagined, his slumbers were very disturbed. He was still, in his dreams, stumbling over coffins and battling with floods. He dreamed of a precipice towards which he was being irresistibly hurried. He struggled wildly in this terrible nightmare and woke with a cry of terror as he felt himself falling through the hole in the floor, towards which he had rolled in his disturbed sleep. He fell with a splash into the water which flooded the room below. However, his fall was broken by his landing on a soft substance. Putting out his hand to feel what he had fallen upon, he withdrew it with horror for it had touched the face of a dead man.

'Good God!' he cried, in terror, 'are the horrors of this night never to cease?'

He staggered to his feet and when he had recovered from the great shock he had received, he struck a match and holding it down saw, staring up at him through the surrounding darkness, the ghastly dead face of poor Mr Campbell, made still more horrible by the look of wild terror that death had frozen on it.

'The widow's curse has been fulfilled,' said Macneil, trembling and shaking with fear yet afraid to move. Thus he stood for what seemed to him a long time till at last the cold, grey light of coming day diffused itself over the pitiable scene. But the faint light only increased poor Macneil's terror for it only served to make darkness visible; and his over-strained imagination saw spectres on every side, while he could not take his eyes off the pale face of his late master, gleaming ghastly through the struggling light of early morn.

'If I do not get out of this I shall go mad,' said he at last, and made an effort to throw off a sensation of dread which chained him to the ground. Taking a step forward he stumbled over some heavy object and fell, striking his head against some furniture so severely that for a time he lay quite stunned. When he recovered, the daylight was strong enough to him to see plainly his dread surroundings. On raising himself and turning to see what had caused his fall, he nearly lost his senses again with horror for what did he see but the body of Mr Campbell with the head supported on a coffin, the broken lid of which revealed to his terror-stricken view the mangled remains of the widow Cameron.

'It is a judgement from heaven,' he exclaimed; 'better for me to drown outside than to stay among these horrors.' So saying he rushed out of the door and half wading, half swimming, he managed at length to reach the road leading to his own house. But as soon as he felt himself on firm ground and in the open daylight, he fell insensible to the ground, utterly worn out with the varied emotions and dangers he had encountered. Thus he was found by some neighbours soon afterwards and carried home, where he kept to his bed for some weeks, suffering from the effects of his exposure and fright during that never-to-be-forgotten night.

When the sun rose on Glenfalcon its rays illuminated as sad a scene as could well be found. The graveyard and the bridge had been carried away by the mad torrent, which tore up every object in its destructive career. Several of the crofters' houses were levelled with the ground. Dead sheep and cattle were to be seen floating amid the waste of water; some were even washed right out into the bay. Mr Campbell's house was a complete wreck, and around it lay scattered the contents of the graveyard. Coffins lay around in all directions, many of them broken, revealing their ghastly contents in all stages of decomposition. Human bones and skulls lay all around too, but the most fearful sight was inside the house where people found Mr Campbell lying, as Macneil described, with his head pillowed on the coffin of the victim of his cruelty.

A feeling of intense awe crept over the people at this fearful sight. 'It is a judgement,' was the universal verdict as they recalled the widow's curse. The excitement went down with the flood. The dead bodies were collected and reinterred, and things resumed their normal course. A new and more substantial bridge was built, and the estate passed into the hands of a distant relative of Mr Campbell, who had the ruins of the ill-fated house levelled with the ground.

It is years since these events happened, but they are still fresh in the memory of the old people in the district who yet relate the story of the dreadful flood, and some aver that the widow's curse still hangs over the place where the proprietor's house once stood, and that on dark stormy nights, when the wind howls mournfully through the glen, the sheeted dead leave their graves to mingle their ghostly voices with the storm.

'The Evicted Widow', published in *The Celtic Magazine*, 1885.

THE WATER KELPIE OF LOCH NESS

The Water Kelpie of Loch Ness

In former and darker ages of the world when people had not half the wit and sagacity they now possess, and when, consequently, they were much more easily duped by such designing agents, the water-horse, or kelpie as it is commonly called, was a well-known character in Scotland. The kelpie was an infernal agent, retained in the service and pay of Satan, who granted him a commission to execute such services as appeared profitable to his interest. He was an amphibious character and generally took up his residence in lochs and pools bordering on public roads and other situations, most convenient for his professional calling.

His commission consisted in the destruction of human beings, without affording them time to prepare for their immortal interests, and thus endeavour to send their souls to his master, while he, the kelpie, enjoyed the body. However, he had no authority to touch a human being of his own free accord, unless the latter was the aggressor. In order, therefore, to delude the public travellers and others to their destruction, it was the common practice of the kelpie to assume the most fascinating form and adapt himself to that likeness which he supposed most congenial to the inclinations of his intended victim.

The likeness of a fine riding-steed was his favourite disguise. Decked out in the most splendid riding accoutrements, the perfidious kelpie would place himself in the weary traveller's way, and graze by the roadside with all the seeming innocence and simplicity in the world. The traveller supposing this fine horse to have strayed from his master, and considering him as a good catch for carrying him a part of the way, would approach the horse with the greatest caution, soothing it with *proogy proogy* and many other terms of endearment, in the event of his taking to his heels, as wild horses are sometimes apt to do. But this horse knew better what he was about; he was as calm and peaceable as a lamb, until his victim was once fairly mounted on his back. Then, with a fiend-like yell he would announce his triumph and, plunging headlong with his woe-struck rider into an adjacent pool, enjoy him for his repast.

One such water kelpie lived in Loch Ness and committed the most atrocious excesses on the defenceless inhabitants of the surrounding districts. It was the common practice of this iniquitous kelpie to prowl about the public roads, decked out in all the trappings of a riding-horse, and in this disguise place himself in the way of the traveller, who often took it into his head to mount him, to his no small prejudice, for upon this the vicious brute would immediately fly into the air and in a jiffy light with his rider in Lochnadorb, Lochspynie, or Loch Ness, where he would enjoy his victim at his leisure.

Filled with indignation at the kelpie's practices, Mr James Macgrigor, a man of great strength and courage, ardently wished to fall in with his kelpieship in order to have a bit of communing with him touching his notorious practices. And Providence, in its wise economy, thought it meet that Mr Macgrigor should be gratified in his wish.

One day as he was travelling along Slochd Muichd, a wild and solitary pass on the road between Strathspey and Inverness, whom did he observe but this identical water kelpie, browsing away by the roadside with the greatest complacency, thinking no doubt, in his mind, that he would kidnap Mr Macgrigor as he had done others. But in this idea he found himself woefully mistaken! For no sooner did Mr Macgrigor espy him than he instantly determined to have a trial of his mettle.

Accordingly, marching up to the horse, who thought, no doubt, he was coming to mount him, Mr Macgrigor soon convinced him of the contrary by drawing his trusty sword with which he dealt the kelpie such a pithy blow on the nose, as almost felled him to the ground. The stroke maltreated the kelpie's jaw very considerably, cutting through his bridle, in consequence of which, one of the bits fell down on the ground. Observing the bit lying at his feet, Mr Macgrigor had the curiosity to pick it up, while the astonished kelpie was recovering from the effects of the blow, and this bit Mr Macgrigor carelessly threw into his pocket. He then prepared for a renewal of his conflict with its former owner, naturally supposing the kelpie would return him his compliment. But what was Mr Macgrigor's surprise when he found that, instead of retorting his blow and fighting out the matter to the last, the

kelpie commenced a cool dissertation upon the injustices and illegality of Mr Macgrigor's proceedings.

'What is your business with me, Mr Macgrigor? I have often heard of you as a man of great honour and humanity. Why, therefore, thus abuse a poor defenceless animal like me? Let me be a horse, or let me be a kelpie, so long as I do you no harm. In my humble opinion, Mr Macgrigor,' continued the kelpie, 'you acted both cruelly and illegally; and certainly your conduct would justify me, if I should return you twofold your assault upon me. However, I abominate quarrels of this sort,' said the conciliatory kelpie, 'and if you peaceably return me the bit of my bridle, we shall say no more on the subject.'

To this learned argument of the kelpie Mr Macgrigor made no other reply than flatly denying his request in the first place and in the second place mentioning in pretty unqualified terms his opinion of his character and profession. 'It is true,' replied the other, 'that I am what you call a kelpie; but it is known to my heart, that my profession was never quite congenial to my feelings. We kelpies engage in many disagreeable undertakings. But, as the proverb says, "Necessity knows no law", and there is no profession that a man or spirit will not sometimes try for the sake of an honest livelihood. So you will please have the goodness to give me the bit of my bridle.'

Observing the great anxiety evinced by the kelpie to have the bit of his bridle restored to him and feeling anxious to learn its properties, the sagacious Mr Macgrigor immediately concocted a plan, whereby he might elicit from the poor dupe of a kelpie an account of its virtues. 'Well, Mr Kelpie,' said Mr Macgrigor, 'all your logic cannot change my opinion of the criminality of your profession, though I confess, it has somewhat disarmed me of my personal hostility to you as a member of it. I am, therefore, disposed to deliver up to you the bit of your bridle, but it is on this express condition that you will favour me with an account of its use and qualities, for I am naturally very curious, do you know?'

To this proposition the kelpie joyfully acceded and thus addressed Mr Macgrigor: 'My dear sir, you must know that such agents as I are invested by our Royal Master with a particular commission consisting of some document delivered to us by his own hand. The commission delivered to a kelpie consists of a bridle invested with all those powers of transformation, information, and observation necessary for our calling; and whenever we lose this commission, whether voluntarily or by accident, our power is at an end and certain annihilation within four and twenty hours is the consequence. Had it not been that my bridle was broken by your matchless blow, I must be so candid as to declare I might have broken every bone in your body: but now you are stronger than myself, and you can be half a kelpie at your pleasure, only please to look through the holes of the bit of the bridle, and you will see myriads of invisible agents, fairies, witches and devils, all flying around you, the same as if you had been gifted with the Second Sight, and all their machinations clearly exposed to your observation.'

'My dear sir,' replied Macgrigor, 'I am much obliged to you for your information. But I am sorry to inform you that your relation has so endeared the bit of your bridle to myself, that I have resolved to keep it for your sake. I could not persuade myself to part with it for any consideration whatever.'

'What!', exclaimed the petrified kelpie, 'Do you really mean, in the face of our solemn agreement, to retain the bit of my bridle?'

'I not only mean it but I am resolved on it,' replied Macgrigor, who immediately proceeded to make the best of his way home with the bit. The kelpie still continued his earnest entreaties, interlarded with anecdotes of great squabbles which he had formerly had with as powerful characters as Mr Macgrigor and which always ended to his eminent advantage but which, he politely insinuated, he would be sorry to see repeated. But when they arrived in sight of Mr Macgrigor's house, his grief and despair for his bridle began to evince themselves in a threatening aspect, but a single flourish of Mr Macgrigor's trusty sword disarmed him of all his might and made him calm as a cat.

At length, when they arrived at Mr Macgrigor's house, his grief and despair for his bridle became perfectly outrageous. Galloping off before Mr Macgrigor, the kelpie told him as he went that he and the bit should never pass his threshold together, and in pursuance of this assurance, he planted himself in Mr Macgrigor's door, summoning up all his powers for the impending conflict.

However, James Macgrigor resolved, if possible, to evade the kelpie's decree, and accordingly going to a back window in his house, he called his wife towards him and threw the bit of the kelpie's bridle into her lap. He then returned to the kelpie, who stood sentry at his door, and told him candidly he was a miserable legislator; for that, in spite of his decree, the bit of his bridle was that moment in his wife's hands.

The kelpie, now finding himself fairly outwitted, saw the vanity of contending with James Macgrigor and his claymore for what could not be recovered. As there was a rowan cross above the door, his kelpieship could no more enter the house than he could pass through the eye of a needle, and he therefore thought it best to take himself off, holding forth, at the same time, in the most beastly language.

Let me remind you what the loss of the bit meant to the poor kelpie. As he had informed Mr Macgrigor, the loss of the bridle or indeed any part of it meant the loss of his powers and certain annihilation within four and twenty hours. Now if this story be true, those who claim to have seen a monster in Loch Ness in recent times must surely be mistaken.

The Popular Superstitions and Festive Amusements, by William Grant Stewart, 1851.

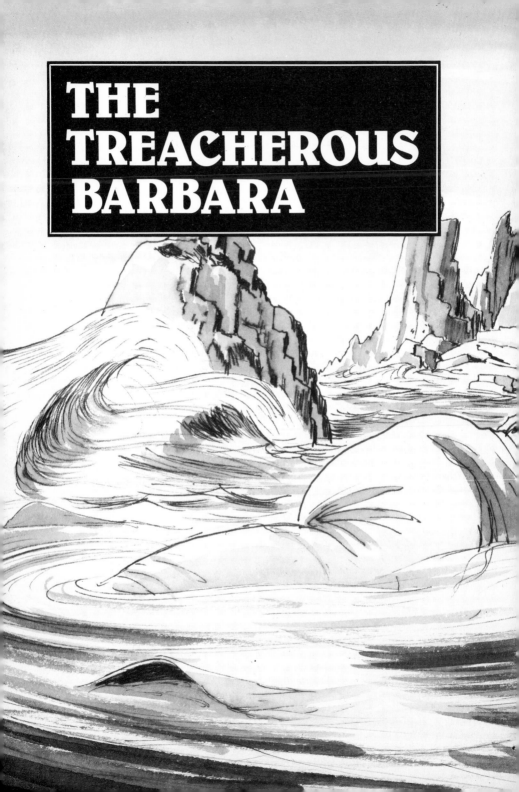

THE TREACHEROUS BARBARA

The Treacherous Barbara

On a dark tempestuous night about the middle of the last century an anxious group of people gathered on the seashore of a small village on the west coast of Argyllshire. In spite of the howling wind and pelting rain they stood, straining their eyes seaward to watch through the gloom the struggles of a gallant ship which, with her devoted crew, seemed doomed to destruction.

The vessel was evidently disabled and totally unmanageable, and the villagers listened with deep emotion and cries of horror and distress to the deep booming of the minute gun and the hoarse cries of the sailors imploring the assistance of those on shore, who were powerless to assist them. Nearer and nearer the ill-fated ship was driven to the deadly rocks, until at length the end came. With a fearful crash she struck; one moment she was lifted high by the cruel waves, the next saw her dashed to pieces like a toy in the hands of a giant, and her crew battling for life in the raging sea.

Now the brave landsmen do their utmost to help. With encouraging shouts they rush through the boiling surf and throw ropes to the drowning men, but alas, few indeed can they save. The women are not idle; they have blankets to throw around the senseless forms, and restoratives to hold to the pallid lips of the half-drowned men. Among the most active was a widow, who with her two daughters was busily engaged in assisting a fine stalwart young sailor just rescued from the waves – whether dead or alive could hardly be ascertained at first. The widow's cottage being near, they conveyed him there, and by their united and sustained efforts had at length the pleasure of seeing him revive and able to thank them for their kindness.

When recovered sufficiently to give an account of his ship and her disastrous voyage, it came out that he belonged to the next village, although he had been absent at sea for several years. They knew his mother well, and great was the joy of all when on the morrow they accompanied him to her house, and related the story of the wreck and his deliverance.

Donald Ban (for such was his name) finding his father was dead and his mother getting frail and requiring help on her small croft, decided to give up a seafaring life and to settle at home. Naturally enough he often paid a visit to the widow's cottage, where he had met with such kindness, but it would be difficult to prove that his visits would have been quite so frequent or prolonged had it not been for the attraction of the widow's daughters, Mary and Barbara.

Mary, the eldest, was a quiet, kind-hearted, sensible girl, with a homely face only rendered attractive by good-nature and robust health. Her one point of beauty lay in her magnificent fair hair which, when released from its fastenings, fell in luxuriant masses down to her feet. Her sister, five years her junior, was a great contrast both in appearance and disposition. Very beautiful in person, lively in manner, she captivated all who came within her power. All the young men for miles around were her devoted admirers, but Barbara was a coquette, and no one knew whom she favoured most. An acute observer might notice that her eyes, bright and beautiful as they were, yet had a cold hard look, and that her cherry lips at times would grow thin and white and wreath into a cruel smile, anything but pleasant to see.

Donald Ban, like the rest, was dazzled by her beauty and attractive manner; at the same time the best part of his nature made him feel that Mary was superior in every true womanly quality to her more fascinating sister. Still he wavered, fluttering like a moth round the light that would finally destroy him. His mother, who was now growing very infirm, wished him to marry and, having known Mary from childhood, was most anxious that Donald should choose her for his wife.

Donald, returning home one evening after a more than usually prolonged visit to the widow's cottage, was alarmed to find his mother lying back in her chair in a swoon. Blaming himself severely for his neglect in leaving her so long alone, he did his utmost to restore her to consciousness. After a little while she somewhat revived, but was evidently very much shaken and ill. Feeling near her end, she spoke very seriously to Donald about his choice of a wife and assured him that while lying apparently unconscious, she had a vision and saw, through the medium of Second Sight, a forecast of the future of the two sisters.

'I saw Mary a happy wife and mother, a blessing and a comfort to her husband, but Barbara's future was dark and sinful. Her lover will be driven by her into the commission of a terrible crime, and both will perish in a sudden and terrible manner. The form of Mary's husband, as also that of Barbara's lover, was hidden from me. But remember this warning. Shun Barbara as you would a beautiful but deadly serpent. Promise me that as soon as I am dead and the days of your mourning are past, you will marry Mary and be a true and faithful husband to her.'

Donald, much affected by his mother's earnest appeal, promised faithfully to carry out her last wishes.

The old woman died shortly after, and in course of time Donald prepared to fulfil his promise. He proposed to Mary and was accepted, her mother being well pleased to have Donald for a son-in-law. Whatever Barbara's feelings were on the subject, she kept them to herself, merely excusing herself from being present at the wedding, by saying that she was going to pay a long visit to a relative in a neighbouring town.

Donald and Mary were married and lived quietly and happily for nearly three years. They had two children, a boy and a girl. Mary's mother dying about this time and Barbara being still unmarried, she came to live with them. She was if possible more beautiful than ever – still in the first bloom of her womanhood; and soon Donald found himself as much under her influence as ever. Manfully he struggled for a time to subdue his fatal passion, but in a short while he was as helpless as a fly in a spider's web. His infatuation was complete, and it made him oblivious to the sacred claims of a husband and father. It is doubtful whether Barbara really felt any affection for him, though withal she used such tact that neither her true-hearted sister nor the unfaithful Donald, ever suspected her.

One lovely summer day Donald was working on his croft close by his cottage. The door was open and exposed a scene of homely comfort. The room was scrupulously clean. Mary, with a happy contented look lighting up and beautifying her homely face, was busily employed making oatcake. A fine collie, basking in the sun outside the door and occasionally lifting his head, would give a satisfied sniff at the appetising smell but was too well-bred to show any impatience. The eldest child, a sturdy boy of two years, was on the floor playing with a kitten, as frolicsome as himself. The baby girl was sleeping in her cradle. Barbara was sitting quietly, knitting.

The humming of the bees as they flitted from flower to flower, the twittering of the birds, and the soothing sound of the waves breaking gently against the neighbouring rocks, completed this picture of peaceful happiness from which discord and trouble seemed far removed. After finishing at the stove, Mary proposed to go to the rocks to gather dulse, of which Donald was very fond. The boy clamoured to go along with her but his mother quieted him by promising to take him out on her return.

Anxious to obtain the best dulse, Mary scrambled on to a rock jutting out in the sea and always covered at high water. Having filled her basket, she sat down to rest, and the day being hot soon fell asleep.

The duties and simple pleasure of domestic life had no attraction for Barbara. She soon tired of being alone and, giving the sagacious dog charge of the children, went to look for her sister. She soon discovered her still peacefully sleeping on the fatal rock. The tide was just turning, but instead of awakening her sister, Barbara stood and stared, and as she looked, an evil flash came in her eye, a cruel smile was on her lips, and from a beautiful woman she seemed suddenly as if transformed into a she-demon.

At length she turned, and going to Donald prevailed upon him to accompany her to the beach, saying she wished to show him something remarkable. Arriving at the rock, she pointed out the still slumbering Mary, and without a word fixed her flashing eyes on Donald. Spellbound he gazed at her, until the same dreadful idea also possessed him. The water was now within a yard of the peaceful and sleeping woman; in a few minutes she would be totally surrounded by the tide, and if not awakened instantly, her life would be lost; yet still they stood silent and inactive.

At last Barbara muttered, or rather hissed, through her close-set teeth, 'We must not let this chance escape; we must make sure work of it. Come, Donald, help me to plait her hair with the sea weeds, and so saying she drew the infatuated man in the direction of his devoted wife.

With eager fingers they quickly unwound poor Mary's long tresses, and plaited and knotted them with the weeds growing on the rock. Then retiring to a point of safety they awaited the inevitable result. The tide had completely surrounded their victim, who as it touched her woke with a start. Donald's heart now failed him. Although he wished her dead, he could not bear to see her murdered. With a groan he turned and fled, stopping his ears for fear of hearing the death agonies of his wife. Barbara looked at him with a scornful smile on her lips and muttered a curse on his cowardice. She did not intend to lose sight of her victim.

When Mary awoke she strove to rise and escape, but to her horror found herself bound to the rock. Startled and confused by her sudden awakening, she imagined for a moment that she was dreaming or under the influence of a dreadful nightmare; but the cold waves breaking over her soon convinced her of her true position. With frantic hands she tore at her hair, crying loudly for help; then catching sight of her sister a gleam of hope came, but to her indescribable horror and despair her cries for assistance were met only with a low mocking laugh. Then was the fearful conviction forced upon her that she was being murdered and at the hands of her own sister. With heart-rending cries she called on her husband to succour her, but the only answer came from Barbara, telling her how he also had even helped to bind her to the rock.

Surprise and horror closed poor Mary's lips for a moment; she then thought of her children – her handsome boy, her firstborn – and her sweet babe, who was even then requiring its natural food. The thought was distraction. Again she tried to move the stony heart of her unnatural sister by pitiable appeals for dear life, imploring her by every tie human and divine to save her; by the memory of their dead mother, by their sisterhood, for the sake of the children, for the sake of her own soul, not to commit this foul deed. But as well might she attempt to stay the tide now washing over her as move the heartless she-fiend who sat gloating over the sight of her victim's sufferings, like a tiger over the struggles of his prey. Inch by inch the water rises, now it reaches her neck, the next wave drowns her voice, there is a gasp and a gurgle. Another wave – the fair head is covered, and poor Mary is in eternal rest.

By Mary's death an obstacle was removed from the path of the guilty pair, but yet they were not happy. Nothing prospered with Donald – his harvest was bad, his potatoes diseased, his sheep died, his cows sickened; however hard he might work, everything went wrong – he got no sympathy nor help from his neighbours, who had all shunned him since his wife's death. He grew gloomy and morose; tortured with remorse, he dragged out a miserable existence. Barbara was also changed – she was never fitted for home duties, and having now no object in trying to captivate Donald, she grew careless and neglectful, and the guilty pair passed most of their time in mutual accusations and recriminations.

The first anniversary of Mary's death arrived. It was a heavy oppressive day, and Donald felt more than usually depressed and miserable. His crime weighed heavily upon his conscience, and his mother's prophetic warning continually rang in his ears. His day's work over he entered his cottage for the night, but how changed it had become – no comfort, no happiness. Instead of a true-hearted loving wife to welcome him there was this woman, beautiful indeed, but she seemed possessed with a mocking devil. Totally heartless herself, she laughed him to scorn whenever he ventured to express regret for the past or hint at amendment in the future. As night drew near, the air became still more oppressive and clouds, heavy with electricity, hung low down; the distant mutterings of thunder were heard, and the forked lightning flashed over the dark and troubled sea.

Donald and Barbara retired to rest, but he at least could not sleep – he felt a presentiment of coming evil. As the storm drew nearer and increased in intensity, he literally quaked with fear. Just at midnight, a terrific thunder clap burst over the house, and as the lurid flash lighted up the room, he saw with unspeakable horror the figure of his murdered wife standing by the bedside. With a severe yet sorrowful look and voice she seemed to say, 'Your hour is come; retribution has overtaken you and your partner in guilt. I go to protect my beloved offspring.' The figure then slowly glided into the next room in which slept the innocent children. Again the thunder pealed long and loud – again the lightning flashed – for a moment a blinding sheet of flame appeared to envelope the cottage. Suddenly, the storm ceased, dying away in distant rumblings of thunder.

Next morning was calm and clear. The people of the neighbourhood were astir by break of day to see what mischief the unusually severe storm had done. Upon arriving at Donald's cottage, they stood struck with astonishment which on further investigation was turned into a feeling of terror. One end of the cottage had been struck by lightning and was a total ruin. Under the scorched rafters lay two blackened and repulsive bodies only just recognisable as the disfigured remains of Donald and his guilty paramour. The other half of the cottage was unscathed, and entering it they found the two lovely children, locked in each other's arms, breathing the breath of innocence and calmly sleeping with that angelic smile and beautiful expression always observed on the face of slumbering infancy. Thus was Mary avenged.

'A Legend of Argyll', published in *The Celtic Magazine*, 1878.

A WEE BIT PROPERTY

A Wee Bit Property

There is a savage magnificence to the cliffs which skirt the northern entrance to the Moray Firth. They present a loftier and more unbroken wall of rock than do the cliffs to the south. During the storms of winter the waves often rise more than a hundred feet against its precipices and at this season we may hear for miles within the bay the sea's savage roar as it lashes the cliffs and caverns. Spire-like crags rise along the base of these cliffs and these are deeply holed, bored by the action of the waves. Here, too, many natural fissures in the rock have been hollowed into immense caverns.

Sometime early in the reign of Queen Anne a fishing yawl, after vainly labouring for hours in a strong gale was forced, at nightfall, to seek shelter on this borbidding shore. On board the yawl was an old fisherman and his son. For hours they had been drenched by spray and chilled by the piercing wind. Their last tack brought them close in to the mouth of a huge cavern and they saw the red glow of a fire lighting up its vast interior and a boat drawn up on the beach.

'See the fire, lad?' shouted the old man above the shrieking of the wind, 'It must be some of the Tarbet fishermen.'

'But see!' yelled the son, 'if I am not mistaken, that's the boat of Uncle Eachen of Tarbet and he is no friend of ours but the storm is getting worse and we have no choice but to make a landing.'

The sea was comparatively calm under the lee of the precipice as he leaped ashore holding the headrope which he quickly secured round a jutting rock then, grabbing the old man's arm, he half lifted him from the boat. The two boatmen picked their way over the smooth and slippery rocks at the mouth of the cave as flakes of snow that had just begun to fall swirled about them.

By the light of the fire within the cave they could see that the place was occupied by three men whom they recognised at once; two of them young and ordinary looking, the third a savage-looking old man of great muscular strength although long past his prime. A keg of spirits placed before them served as a table upon which stood little tin measures. The mask-like expressions of the younger men showed that they had been indulging freely, but the elder looked comparatively sober.

As the two men entered, the three by the fire started to their feet, and one of the younger, laying hold of the little cask, pitched it hurriedly into a dark corner of the cave.

'Aye, ye do well to hide it, boy!' exclaimed old Eachen, 'here are our good friends William and Ernest Beth come to rob us once again.'

For years the crew of the little fishing yawl had been regarded with the bitterest hatred by the temporary inmates of the cave; nor was old Eachen of Tarbet one whose resentments may be safely slighted. His hard cold eyes and sneeringly sinister countenance betrayed his soul. He had spent much of his life among the buccaneers of South America and in more recent times he had been engaged in the smuggling trade which, even at this early date, was rife on the eastern coasts of Scotland. He had returned from America at a time when the country was engaged in one of its long wars with Holland.

William Beth, the elder fisherman who had served in the English fleet, had been lying at the time in a Dutch prison, and his family believed him to be dead. William had inherited some property from his father – a house and a little field and in his absence it was occupied by his sister, who on the report of his death, was of course regarded as a village heiress, a woman of property, and consequently considered far more desirable as a wife by the few middle-aged bachelors of the village. Eachen of Tarbet had courted this lady and soon they were married. But marriage to this dissipated, cruel man had brought her nothing but heartache. After giving birth to two boys, the younger inmates of the cave, she had died broken in health and spirit. Her brother William had returned from Holland shortly before, and on her death claimed and recovered his property from her husband; and from that hour Eachen of Tarbet had regarded him with the bitterest of hatred.

A second cause of dislike had but recently occurred. Ernest Beth, William's only son, and one of his cousins, the younger son of Eachen, had both fixed their affections on a lovely young girl, the toast of a neighbouring parish; and Ernest, a handsome and high-spirited young man, had proved the successful lover. On returning with this girl from a fair, only a few weeks previous to this evening, he had been waylaid and grossly insulted by his two cousins. The insults to himself he could perhaps have borne but they had also insulted the girl whose company he kept, and this he could not bear; and so he had beaten the two. So thoroughly did he beat them that it was several days before they were fit to take their place once more in their father's boat.

William Beth had heard the insulting remark made by Eachen as he had entered the cave but he chose to ignore it. 'Well, Eachen, I did not expect to be meeting you, but fate and the storm has brought us to this meeting and if you have no objection we should be obliged for a seat by your fire.'

'There's no end to the mischief that such a storm can do' said Eachen, 'No knowing what foul flotsam it may spew on to the shore.' He had resumed his seat by the fire and without further exchange the old fisherman and his son sat down opposite him, while Eachen's two sons skulked in the shadows at the rear of the cave.

'It is foolish that our young folk should not be on friendly terms,' said the old fisherman, 'Our quarrels are not their quarrels.' Old Eachen made no reply but stared fixedly into the fire. 'We ourselves should be on friendly terms, too,' continued the fisherman. 'We are old men now, Eachen, with too little time left to be wasting it on fighting and feuding.'

Eachen raised his eyes from the fire and fixed his cold, disdainful gaze upon the speaker. 'Ye have robbed my boys o' the wee bit property that would have come to them from their mother,' he snarled, 'and no content wi' this, ye send your son to murder them; to waylay them in the dark and brutally beat two young innocent boys. What more can ye want o' us? But I'm thinking, maybe ye came here this night to settle an old score once and for all; "old Eachen and his sons lost in the storm and drowned"; is that the way of it, William Beth?'

Ernest Beth could stay silent no longer, he rose quickly to his feet, flushed with anger. 'I had no wish to raise my hand against my cousins, Uncle, and I dare either of them to say the quarrel was of my seeking. As to our little property, that was my grandfather's and of right descended to his only son.'

'Wheesht, Ernest,' said his father, 'Sit ye down. More than twenty years have passed since we quarrelled over yon bit o' property,' said the old fisherman, addressing Eachen once more. 'More than twenty years since we laid my poor sister to rest. Ye were no the best o' husbands,

Eachen. You're o'er fond o' the spirits and even when sober ye have the temper of a crab. Maybe this can be accounted for by having gone through hard times when ye were young, but I too have my faults and weaknesses. You and I are now nearing the end o' the road, but these boys have scarcely begun the journey. If we old dogs are too old to change, we can at least see to it that we don't allow this foolish feuding to be continued by our sons.'

Eachen spat into the fire then wiped his mouth on the back of his arm. 'I had hard times in my youth right enough, but my hard times never came to an end, they followed me down through the years. I'm not a lucky man like you, William Beth. My father left me no property. I have had to work, and work hard for every morsel o' bread I've consumed. Aye – and every drop o' spirits that have passed these lips. You've had all the luck, William Beth. Ye have a nice wee rent coming in from yon house and croft. Ye have a wife at home worrying now that ye have nae returned from the sea, and lighting a lantern in the window to guide ye home. But I lost my dear wife, and not content wi' making me a widower, the fates bring ye back from the dead to take from me my house and land. They gave ye a son wi' the strength o' two men to work your boat so that ye can sit back in your old age, but they gave me these two whelps who together dinna equal one man. Drinking and lying in their teeth is what they excel at.'

He turned to his sons who were sitting at the back of the cave passing the keg of spirits from one to the other, and now he addressed them in heavily sarcastic tone. 'Come here and tell me again what happened the night ye returned home bleeding from a beating administered by your cousin. Come face the man ye accused and, if ye repeat one – just one o' the lies ye told me then – I'll cut the livers from ye and use them to bait the hooks!'

Neither of the two young men made any effort to rise, and in their condition of drunkenness it is doubtful if they could have succeeded in doing so had they tried. Old Eachen had obviously not expected them to obey his command because he immediately addressed himself to William Beth once more. 'It would have been better if ye had died at the hands o' yon Dutchmen and not returned to plague me and mine. Ye claim ye want friendship, but ye list my faults like ye were the Almighty sitting in judgement. 'Tis easy for a man who is favoured in this world to find fault wi' the less fortunate. I dinna want your friendship, William Beth. I want what is rightfully mine, and that will not come to me by friendship.'

Ernest Beth's patience was at an end and he rose to his feet saying, 'Come, father, we would do better to face the storm.' He took his father by the arm and assisted him to his feet. The storm had not abated, and they hesitated at the entrance to the cave, reluctant to leave its shelter. There was no leaving this place by land for the cliffs were sheer and impossible to climb, and the beach ran only a short distance before it was obstructed by pinnacles of rock rising to a great height preventing any escape by that route. They struggled with the boat until they had it riding a short distance from the shore but still attached by the hawser to the rocks; then they lay in the bottom of the boat with the sail covering them and slept fitfully.

The wind moderated next day, and in the afternoon Eachen and his sons returned to Tarbet; but the yawl of William Beth was not seen in the Bay of Cromarty. The wife of William Beth kept an anxious vigil all that day and by nightfall she had seen all the fishermen caught in the storm return to the village. All, that is, but her husband and son. When the wife questioned the other fishermen none had seen her husband's yawl, but they tried to reassure her, telling her confidently that the two were good seamen and would return safe and sound the following day. Even when that day had passed without sight nor word of the two men, they were still voicing their confidence and suggesting that the yawl would have made a landing at some other port.

In the days that followed these men searched all likely places where a boat might have been washed ashore, and the clergyman in the village made enquiries regarding the missing fishermen all along the firth, but it seemed that they had disappeared without trace. Eventually all hope for their safe return began to fade. The widow went into mourning, and old Eachen lost no time in claiming the house and the little field on behalf of his sons.

In the years that followed the disappearance of her husband and son, the poor widow lived in grief and poverty. Her only consolation was the friendship of the young girl whom her son had courted. The sorrow that they shared in the loss of Ernest formed a strong bond between the two, and a day never went by without the girl, Helen Henry, paying a visit to the widow's cottage.

The widow's health had never been robust, and now she became so feeble that she was often confined for days to her bed. The cottage, however, bore witness to the daily efforts of her young friend. Everything was neat and tidy and a good fire blazed on a clean, comfortable-looking hearth.

One day in late autumn and five years after the disappearance of the fishermen, Helen was paying her customary visit to the widow's home. The day had been gloomy and lowering, and as the evening advanced a tremendous sea began to roll ashore.

'The gulls have been flying landward since daybreak,' said the widow, 'And I have never seen the sea break so heavily against the shore. My heart goes out to the poor sailors who must bide under it all.'

'Aye,' said Helen, 'I canna sleep at nights for thinking o' them, when it is stormy like this, though I have no one to bind me to them now. But, look; yonder is a boat rounding the rock with only one man in it. See how the waves break over its bow!'

'He should no' be out in so small a boat,' said the widow, 'But I think I should ken that boatman. Is it no Eachen of Tarbet?'

'Aye, I think you're right,' replied the maiden. 'He appears to be making for the boat-haven below. What can be bringing that hard-hearted man here? How cruel it was of him to rob you of your little property in the very first days of your grief! He is landing but see how worn out he appears. He is having difficulty walking over the rough stones. Oh dear! He has fallen. I must run to his assistance. But, no – he has risen again. See, he is coming straight to the house.'

'I need shelter, Lillias,' he said, addressing the widow. 'Surely ye'll no refuse me on a night like this?'

Eachen was soon seated by the fire which the girl had hurriedly heaped with fresh fuel. Food and ale were brought to him but he ignored it and sat with his hands covering his face. His head was bowed almost to his knees. 'Heaven have mercy on them,' said Eachen in a tremulous voice, 'my two boys are still out there in the firth.'

When she heard this the widow's heart went out to him, in spite of him being who he was. She knew all too well the anxiety and the pain of waiting while loved ones struggled for their lives in a stormy sea. 'May God be merciful and bring them safe ashore,' she said. 'It was on such a night as this that my Ernest perished.' The old man lowered his eyes, groaned, and wrung his hands.

The wind outside made a terrible noise as it buffeted the house, but even so they plainly heard the sound of a gun.

'Some poor vessel in distress,' said the widow, 'but where can help come from on such a night? Only from God. But wait, draw off the cover from the window, Helen, and I'll light the lantern. My poor William has told me how my light has often showed him his bearings and kept him off the rocks.'

They heard the boom of the gun at measured intervals and each shot louder than the last until it seemed that the sound came from the interior of the bay.

'She has entered the bay,' said Helen. 'I can see her lights. She'll be safe now. I think perhaps your light has saved lives this night.'

By morning the wind had dropped and, although a heavy swell continued to break on the shore, the weather was much improved. Old Eachen left the cottage while the two women were still sleeping. He walked down to the boat-haven below the cottage to ensure that his boat was still secure; then he walked along the beach to the east where heaps of kelp and tangle lay, uprooted and washed ashore by the storm. Among the seaweed and the rocks he noticed the scattered fragments of a boat, and he stooped to pick up a piece of the wreck in the fearful expectation of finding some mark by which he might recognise it. Suddenly he started as he recognised instead a human face, horribly swollen and grotesque; pale against the dark green of the seaweed. It was that of his eldest son, and face-down a short distance off lay the body of the younger, broken and torn by having been smashed against the rocks.

Later that morning a young man stood outside the widow's cottage. He lingered there for some time looking slowly about him as though enchanted by all that he saw. Many people had visited the stretch of beach where the wreckage of the boat had been found. Some had helped to carry the bodies from the beach to an old storehouse about a mile to the west of the cottage; but now they had all dispersed, leaving this solitary individual whom no one knew. He was a handsome man of about seven and twenty, dressed in a naval uniform with three narrow stripes of gold on one of the sleeves of his jacket. At length he walked up the path to the cottage door, raised the latch and went in.

Inside the cottage the widow sat beside the fire, her hands covering her face. If she was aware of his entrance she showed no sign of it. Helen Henry was fast asleep. She lay still fully dressed on the bed in a corner of the room. The young man went to stand beside the widow and gently laid his hand upon her shoulder. She started and looked up.

'I have travelled far to bring you news of your missing husband and son,' he said. Before continuing, he drew up a chair close to the widow and seated himself, then he took her hand in his. 'It is now five years since they were blown out to sea by a strong gale from the land. They drifted for four days before being picked up by an armed vessel cruising in the North Sea. Your husband was in a poor state from all the fatigues he had undergone and he did not survive many days. Ernest was better able to endure the hardships and he survived to this day, and I have come to prepare you to meet with him. The ship which had taken him aboard was bound for Spanish America, and the Captain, refusing to attempt a landing on the Scottish mainland in such heavy seas, informed Ernest that he must stay with the ship until they reached their destination.

'But where is Ernest now?' enquired the widow impatiently.

'He is Lieutenant of the vessel whose guns you must have heard during the night,' replied the young man. 'After the ship arrived in Spanish America, Ernest stayed on as a permanent member of the crew and by his own merit has risen to be the second in command. And now he returns home with gold enough to make his old mother comfortable. Last night he saw your light and steered by it into the safety of the bay, blessing you all the way. But tell me, for he anxiously wished me to enquire of you, whether Helen Henry is yet married?'

'Ernest – it is you!' exclaimed Helen rising from the bed. A moment later he had locked her in his arms.

Old Eachen lay tossing and turning in a delirium of fever in the loft of the storehouse. The bodies of his two sons occupied the floor below. The grief and horror of the day had robbed him of his wits. He muttered ceaselessly and occasionally cried out, seemingly convinced in his own demented mind that William and Ernest Beth were there in the room with him. Every time he began to say a prayer for his poor boys and himself, William Beth would clamp his cold swollen hand over his mouth to prevent him from saying the prayer.

'What do you want of me? – you have taken all I held dear – you have taken my poor boys. For five long years you have haunted me, William Beth. How much longer must I suffer it? I did not take your life – I but cut the hawser. It was the storm that killed; the sea that drowned. No – get back – don't touch me! Ye are no match for me with y're cold dead hands.'

At that moment Ernest Beth entered the apartment holding before him a lantern. He could just make out the figure of the old man sprawled in a corner of the dirty room. Ernest bent down and was about to touch the old man when the light from the lantern suddenly lit the young man's face. Eachen instantly recoiled from him with a horrified shriek, 'the old man is weak but the son is strong.' Then he instantly expired.

A traditional tale of Cromarty, first published in 1869 in *Scenes and Legends* by Hugh Miller.

VENGEANCE OF THE SPIRITS

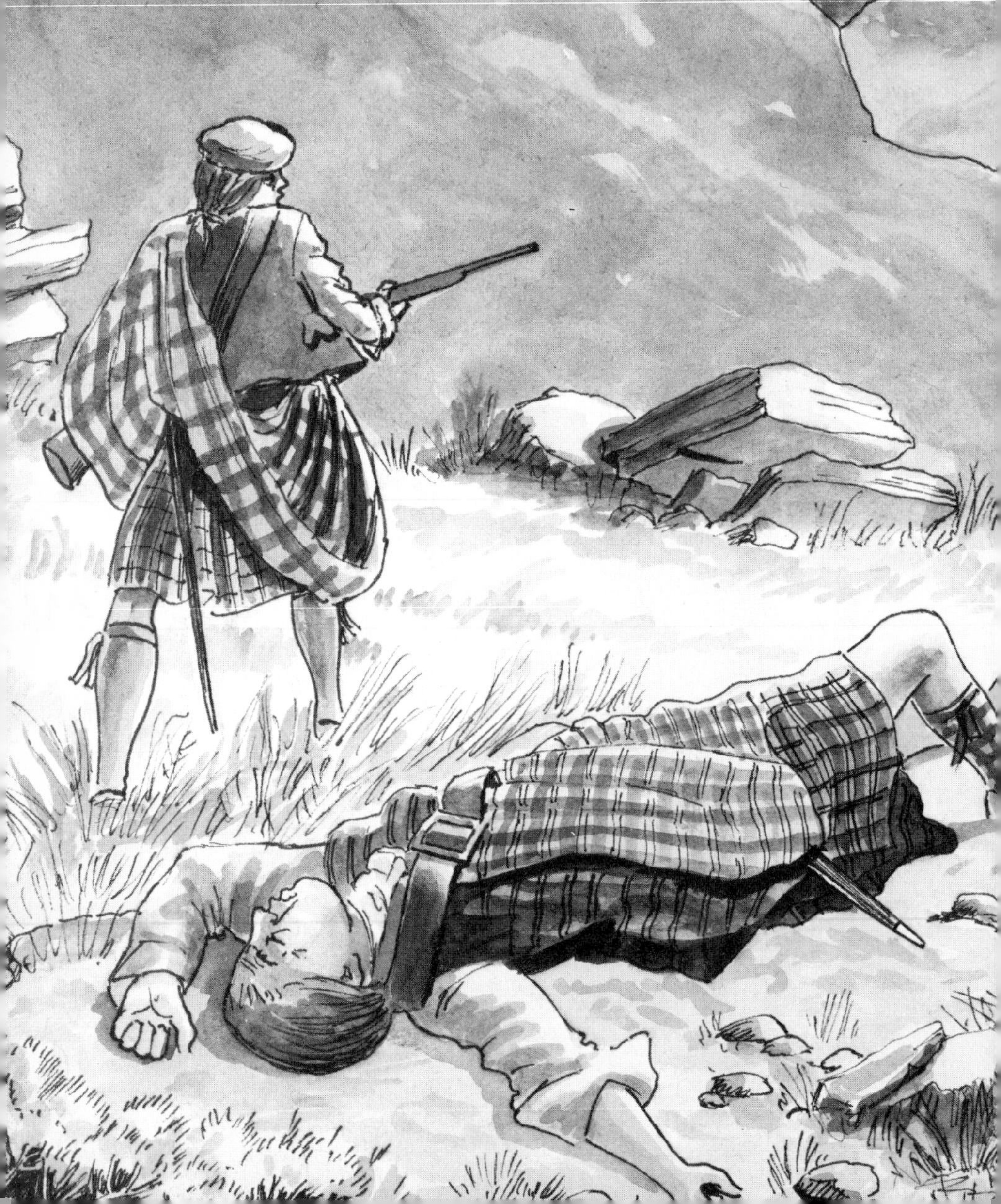

Vengeance of the Spirits

The vengeance of the spirits of the dead who had been wronged was not always supposed to fall upon the person who did the evil. The punishment of the cruelty, oppression or misconduct of an individual might descend as a curse on his children. All ranks were influenced by it; and many believed that if the curse did not fall upon the first or second generation, it would inevitably descend upon the succeeding. The following two stories serve to illustrate this belief.

There were once two drovers of the name Macgregor who had travelled far from their home glen to purchase cattle. One winter's evening found them in Glenquoich and, not being acquainted with the mountain paths in that glen, they called at one of the cottages enquiring after a guide who could lead them safely to their destination. Their knock at the cottage door was answered by a woman, who upon hearing that they needed a guide, immediately called her husband who agreed to act in this capacity, and a price for this service was agreed between them.

The three men travelled by a remote path through the high hills that tower over the western end of Glenquoich. The two Macgregors talked as they walked along and from some remark they made their guide learned that they carried money with them for the purchase of cattle. The dishonest fellow began to plan how he might transfer the coin from their sporrans to his own. Both the Macgregors were armed with muskets, and the guide decided that his first priority must be to somehow disarm the two. This he succeeded in doing by a very cunning device. The Macgregors were weary from their long journey so he asked each one in turn if he might carry his musket for him. Each time he had a musket in his possession he managed to wet it. Carrying the first one he stooped to drink while crossing a stream and as he did so he made sure that the gun received a good ducking. With the second gun he pretended to slip while crossing a boggy place, and again the gun became wet and useless.

The guide often walked behind instead of going before as a guide ought to do, and the Macgregors became suspicious. The one whose musket he carried asked for it to be returned, and the guide handed him the gun with a readiness which convinced the Macgregors of his good faith and so they continued their journey with the guide still bringing up the rear. They had not gone much further when there was a loud report and one of the Macgregors fell mortally wounded. The other turned quickly to see the guide holding a brace of pistols, one of which was smoking from having just been fired. The Macgregor pointed his musket at the treacherous guide but it refused to fire. An instant later the guide fired the second pistol, and both Macgregors lay dead in the heather.

The guide took the money from the men's sporrans before dragging the two bodies off the path to a place on the hillside where there was soft, deep peat in which to bury them. He returned home to live more comfortably with the wealth he had now acquired but sometimes when he was out late in the gloaming he would imagine that he could hear voices calling. They would always repeat the same word over and over – 'Vengeance! Vengeance!' When troubled by the voices he would try to ignore them and seek solace in drinking to excess. One night, however, the voices were louder than usual and could not be ignored. 'Vengeance! Vengeance!', they cried, and defiantly he shouted back, 'Upon whom? Upon whom?' Then the answer came back, 'On the son, the grandson, or the great-grandson!' But the hardened wretch replied, 'If it will go as far off as the great-grandson, I do not care. Let it take its chance.'

Years passed away and at last the murderer died, and his son brought a wife to live with his mother in the old home. One day this young woman went out to the end of the cottage as the shadows of evening were falling upon the hills. Her husband was away from home and she strained her eyes to catch a glimpse of him returning. She could not see him but she saw two stalwart men wearing the Macgregor tartan climbing the mountain above the house on the very path on which her husband should return. She went in and told her mother-in-law, who immediately cried, 'Woe's me! 'tis the Macgregors; the vengeance is to fall upon the son, and you are a widow tonight and I am childless.' The

old woman had always suspected that her husband had murdered the two men. He had returned home too soon on the day of the murder to have conducted the two to their destination and also from that day he had become a wealthy man. She had lived in fear that one day the vengeance of the dead men would fall on a member of the family.

All night long the two women cowered in terror by the hearth, but he for whom they so anxiously waited never returned. His tracks were found in the snow on the hills, but he was never found, and no one doubted but that he had met the Macgregors.

The second story is connected with the Massacre of Glencoe. Captain Robert Campbell and one hundred and twenty men of Argyll's Regiment were billeted in the homes of the people of Glencoe. On the morning of 13 February 1692 the Campbells slaughtered their hosts the MacDonalds in the crime known as the Massacre of Glencoe.

Many years later Colonel Campbell of Glenlyon, a grandson of Robert Campbell, became an officer in the 42nd Regiment. He then entered the Marines. In 1762 he was a Major with the brevet rank of Lieutenant-Colonel and commanded eight hundred of his corps at Havannah. In 1771 he was ordered to superintend the execution of the sentence of a court martial on a soldier of marines, condemned to be shot. A reprieve was sent, but the whole ceremony of the execution was ordered to proceed until the criminal should be upon his knees with a cap over his eyes and ready to receive the volley. It was then that he was to be informed of his pardon. No person was to be told previously, and Colonel

Campbell was directed not to inform even the firing-party, who were warned that the signal to fire would be the waving of a white handkerchief by the commanding officer. When all was prepared, the clergyman having left the prisoner on his knees in momentary expectation of his fate, and the firing-party was looking with close attention for the signal, Colonel Campbell put his hand into his pocket for the reprieve; but in pulling out the packet, the handkerchief accompanied it. They fired, and the unfortunate prisoner was shot dead.

The paper dropped through Colonel Campbell's fingers, and, clapping his hand to his forehead, he exclaimed, 'The curse of God and Glencoe is here; I am an unfortunate ruined man.' He desired the soldiers to be sent to the barracks, instantly quitted the parade, and soon afterwards retired from the Service. This retirement was not the result of any reflection or reprimand on account of this unfortunate affair, as it was known to be entirely accidental, but the impression on his mind was never effaced. Nor is the massacre and the judgement, which the people believe to have fallen on the descendants of the principal actors in this tragedy effaced from their recollection.

FORECAST
OF DEATH

Forecast of Death

Early in the eighteenth century there lived in Dumfries a worthy man of the name Gillespie, who followed the honest though highly unpopular occupation of excise officer or gauger. At the time my story begins he had just been appointed to a new district in the Highlands, and it is while he is on his journey there that we first make his acquaintance. Behold him, then, a tall, thin, ungainly figure, with a consequential self-important air, dressed in a coat of bottle-green cloth with large silver-gilt buttons, a striped yellow waistcoat, corduroy breeches and top boots. A tall peaked hat with narrow brim, a large drab overcoat, and a sword-stick completed his costume. He was mounted on a small shaggy pony or garron, with neither shoes, bit, nor saddle; its head was secured by a Highland bridle made of horsehair, and in lieu of a saddle was a housing of straw mat on which was placed a wooden pack-saddle which had two horn-like projections on which was hung the luggage of the rider.

Having jogged along for some considerable time over a lonely moor without meeting any sign of human habitation, it occurred to Mr Gillespie that he had lost his way. While staring about him for something to guide him, he was nearly dismounted by the sudden starting of the pony, and on pulling up he discovered that he had almost ridden over a young red-headed Highlander lying in the heather and indolently supporting his head on one hand while with the other he leisurely picked the blaeberries that grew so plentifully around him. On seeing what he considered a *Duine-uasal* or Gentleman, the lad started to his feet and, grasping a forelock of his curly hair, made a profound bow.

The rider stared for a moment at the bare-legged, bare-footed, bare-headed figure who had so suddenly appeared, and after stiffly returning his courtesy enquired how far it was to Dunvegan. The other, shaking his head, replied, 'It is to Dunvegan then that you will be going, Sir?'

'Yes, and I am afraid I shall not be able to find my way there without your assistance,' replied Gillespie.

'And maybe you'll be stopping there for some time?' proposed the lad, scratching one bare knee with his sharp, uncut nails as he spoke.

'What does it matter to you, my lad, whether my stay there will be long or short? All I want just now is to get there.'

'Is it far you'll be coming today, sir?' enquired the other with an air of respectful deference strangely inconsistent with the apparent bluntness of the question.

'What business is that of yours? Is it necessary for your showing me the road that I should tell you all my history?'

'Maybe you'll be coming from the change-house of Loch-Easkin?' pursued the youth, without appearing to notice the rebuke of the stranger's reply.

'Maybe I did,' rejoined the gauger dryly, giving a hard blow to the poor garron.

'Good-bye to you,' said the young man, pulling his forelock and bowing as before.

'Why are you in such a hurry to be off all at once before you have shown me the way?' enquired the gauger.

'I'm no in a hurry, sir; I just be doing my work, minding my mother's cow and calf,' answered the lad, lying down again and commencing to pick blaeberries. 'But,' he added, 'it was no' to offend you I was meaning.'

'Offend me, man! For what? I am sure I have taken no offence.'

'Haven't you, sir,' exclaimed the other, jumping up; 'I thought you had, for you didn't seem pleased when I asked what could I be doing for you.'

'My good lad,' answered Gillespie, 'I see customs differ, and what may be considered ill-manners on the streets of Dumfries is perhaps a different thing on a Highland moor, and so I shall be very glad of your company and assistance.'

'Then you must tell me where is it you'll be wanting to go to.'

'Man alive! Have I not told you already I want to reach Dunvegan?'

'But I'm no sure if you're fit to do it before night, if you don't tell me where you came from the day.'

'There is some reason in that,' said the gauger; 'and yet,' he muttered to himself, 'it is a sly way of demonstrating the necessity of his endless questions.'

After going some distance in silence, the boy thinking himself bound to say something, began with, 'You'll be a stranger to this country, Sir?'

'You may say that, man; but what sort of a place is this Dunvegan?'

'It's a bonny place enough, and no want of what's right. The *Uisgebeatha* is plenty, and she's real good; but I doubt it'll no' be so good and so plenty now, for they say that a *sgimilear* of a gauger is coming to live among us; I hope he may break his neck on the way.'

Here Mr Gillespie suddenly saw something amiss with the bridle, which necessitated his bending down for a moment or two and no doubt this accounted for his face being slightly flushed when he raised his head and, giving the unconscious lad an indignant look, said, 'Hem-a-hem! What right has a mere lad like you to speak so disrespectfully of one you never saw and who never harmed you?'

'May his gallows be high and his halter tight!' was the laconic but emphatic reply.

'You young heathen, how dare you say so of a stranger, and without any reason either?'

'Reason in plenty. Is he no' coming to stop us from making our whusky? and there is my Uncle Donald has a still in Craig-bheatha, and my mother helps him to make the malt and gets a piggie [jar] for herself at the New Year; and there's *Somhairle Dubh* at the change-house; he has a still in his barnyard near the ——'

'Hush, friend!' interrupted Gillespie, clapping his hand on the Highlander's mouth, 'dinna betray secrets so.' He then added with great dignity, 'Young man, you have abused me and called me vile names to my face, but for that I forgive you as it was done in ignorance. However, you should be more respectful in referring to His Majesty's revenue service, for I am that very excise officer or gauger, as you call me, appointed by my King and country to watch over the interests of the revenue in this most outlandish corner of his dominions. Heaven help me withal! Now, friend, understand me; I will do my duty without fear, favour, or affection; yes,' he continued, rising to the subject and, to the young man's consternation, drawing his sword and flourishing it over his head, 'Yes, I will do so even unto death; but,' he added after a pause, 'I am no hunter after unguarded information, and God forbid the poor should want their New Year whisky because I am in the parish. But be more discreet in future, for assuredly I must do my duty and grasp, seize, capture, and retain unlawful liquor and implements of its manufacture, whenever I find them, for I am sworn to do this; but,' he concluded, with a bow to his pack-saddle, 'I will always strive to do my duty like a gentleman.'

The boy's emotions during this oration were of a mingled character. At first pure shame was uppermost for having, as he unwittingly discovered he had done, insulted a *Duine-uasal*. Accordingly an honest blush spread over his sun-freckled face and he hung down his head. Then came concern for having, as he apprehended, betrayed the private affairs of his uncle and *Somhairle dubh* into the hands of the spoiler. It was with a feeling of great respect that he replied, repeating his bow, 'I thought you was a *Duine-uasal* from the first, sir, and I beg your pardon a thousand times for foolish words spoke without thinkin', and I could cut my tongue off for having spoke.'

'Friend, that would not be right; no man has a right to maim himself,' said the gauger, as he pulled a box that looked like a large flute-case out of an enormous pocket of his greatcoat. This he opened and, to the admiration of the boy, took out of it first the stock, and then the tube of a short, single-barrelled fowling-piece, which after duly joining together, he went through the process of priming and loading. These preparations were apparently caused by a curlew alighting at a little distance, but which, as if aware that evil was not far away, resumed its flight and soon disappeared.

'She's a very pretty gun indeed, Sir,' began the boy, anxious to renew the conversation on a more agreeable topic than the last. 'By your leave, may I ask where you got her?'

'Got her,' said the other, 'why, I made it, man. In my country we think nothing of making a gun before breakfast.' As this was said with the utmost gravity, the boy was considerably staggered by it for the Highlander, naturally credulous, intending none, suspects no deception, but if a hoax is being played upon him, and he finds it out, he is sure to repay it with interest, and the biter will be keenly bit.

'One before breakfast, Sir! A gun like her made before breakfast!' he repeated, looking anxiously into the other's face, 'surely the thing is just impossible?'

'No, friend,' replied the other, silently chuckling at finding the youth so ductile, 'I tell you, I frequently make one of a morning.'

'Then,' said the guide, 'I suppose, sir, you'll be come to the Highlands to make a big business with them!'

'Maybe, maybe, friend. I daresay there are not many such in this country; but what would still more surprise you, is to hear by whom I was taught the art of making them.'

'Who she'll be, sir?'

'Why, Luno, the son of Leven, who made Fingal's famous sword, which went by his name, and every stroke of which was mortal.'

'Och! yes, Sir,' exclaimed the boy with eyes sparkling, 'ye mean Mac-an-Luinn.'

'But are there any hereabouts who know how to use such a thing as this?' asked the gauger, putting the piece to his eye.

'Och! aye sir; there's Duncan Sealgair can hit a fox or an otter at a hundred yards, easy.'

'I am not speaking,' said the gauger, with an air of sovereign contempt, 'of otters and foxes and such low vermin; I ask you, man, as to shooting of game!'

'Aye, Sir, a good lot of that too. There's old Kenneth Matheson, she'll be very good at killing a buck.'

'Pshaw! man, cannot you get your ideas above coarse four-footed beasts, great sprawling objects that there is no merit in killing.'

The boy scratched his head at a loss what to answer next; but at length with the air of a man who thinks he has made a discovery, exclaimed; 'You'll be meaning the wild goose, Sir!'

'You're a wild goose yourself. I mean no such thing; I am asking ye, man, about grouse, red grouse.'

The guide was as puzzled as if he had heard Hebrew; but just then, as if to relieve his embarrassment, there arose a *Ca, ca* sound in the heather. 'She'll shust be the muir-hens, sir, perhaps you'll like a shot at them.'

'Moor-hens! What's that, lad?', but further explanation was unnecessary, for the eye of the traveller caught the very red grouse he had appeared so anxious to find. The sight seemed to have a very agitating effect upon him, for he instantly stopped, dismounted, and gave his nag to the keeping of his companion; he then crept forward a few paces, his heart beating with the greatness of the occasion.

At length, when he had got closer to the birds than most sportsmen would deem quite necessary, he knelt on one knee and took a most deliberate rifleman-like aim. On placing his finger on the trigger, his face was turned a little to one side – perhaps to avoid the expected smoke. He at length pulled the trigger, but instead of a report there was merely a snap in the pan. At this, the eldest, apparently, of the birds gave a *Ca, ca* and peered about to see what was the matter; and, to avoid being seen, the sportsman sank down among the heather.

Tying the garron to a juniper root, the guide now cautiously crept up and enquired in a whisper, 'Has she refused, sir?'

'Hush!', said the other, shaking his hand for silence, 'has who refused?'

'I mean, Sir,' again whispered the guide, 'has the musket refused?'

'Which, I suppose,' responded the other, 'is as much to say, has it missed fire? Yes, certainly it has; did you not hear the snap in the pan?'

'Yes, sir, but there was no fire; maybe t'was the fault of the flint.'

'Pish, no; there is not a better flint on this side of the Grampians!'

'But the powder, Sir?'

'No better powder in the world, unless it was damped by your horrid Highland mist.'

'There's no' a mist at all the day, Sir,' answered the boy, looking quietly down at the gun lock and discovering for the first time that there was no flint at all. He smiled aside, and then turning to the would-be sportsman, who was kneeling for another attempt, pointed out the circumstance to him. The latter, on seeing it, stared and then added, apparently recollecting himself, 'Dash it, neither there is! I recollect now, here it is. I put it in my waistcoat pocket this morning while cleaning my gun and forgot to fix it again.' So saying, he screwed it tight into its proper place and, kneeling as before, gave a second snap in the pan.

'The priming fell out when she first refused, Sir, and you forgot to put in another.'

'And ye gouck, couldn't you tell me that before?' said the wrathful gauger as he recovered his arms for another attempt. This time, however, he was successful, for his volley levelled the cock leader and two of his family, while the remainder took flight.

'I dare say, friend bare-legs, you do not often see such shots as that in these quarters?'

''Deed, Sir, I'll no' say I do,' returned the other with a look and a manner somewhat equivocal.

'In sooth, I suppose no one hereabouts knows anything of grouse-shooting; but for myself, as I have already said, give me but the birds within tolerable reach and I am sure to hit them.'

'Na doot, Sir, especially if ye always make it a fashion to shoot them sittin'!'

'And have ye any hereabouts that can shoot them any other gait, callant?'

'Maybe, Sir; the young laird, and the minister's son, and the major, and——'

'Weel, Sir, and pray how does the young laird find out the game? Has he any pointers?'

'Pointers, Sir, what's that?' enquired his companion, affecting ignorance.

'You fool, do you not know what a pointer is! Precious country I am come to and perhaps to lay my bones in – not to know what a pointer is!'

'And d'ye ken, Sir, what a bochan is?'

'Not I, friend bare-legs, nor do I care.'

'My name, Sir, is Eachainn. You see there'll be some things that folks who are very clever don't know. A bochan, sir is what you call in Beurla a hobgoblin.'

'I see your drift, man, I see your drift, and care not what a bochan or a fiddlestick means; but a pointer is a dog of right Spanish breed, which has such instinct that he smells out the birds without seeing them, so that when he has got one in a covey within reach of his nose, he holds up his leg and stands stock-still, until his master comes up and blazes away at them.'

'Sitting, Sir?' asked Eachainn, with a roguish look.

'Aye, man, sitting or standing; 'tis all the same.'

All at once they heard the peculiar note of the corn crake or, as it is called in Gaelic, *trian-ri-trian*. The gauger, always anxious to show off his skill as a marksman, began to handle his fowling-piece.

Eachainn looked on with evident uneasiness and at last said, 'Surely, surely, Sir, you'll not be going to shoot her?'

'And why not, my friend?'

'What, Sir! shoot a *trian-ri-trian!* It's just awful to think on!'

'And what is the great harm of shooting such a blethering, craiking thing as that?'

'The harm, Sir! Why, she'll be a sacred bird; I'd as soon think of shooting a cuckoo herself as to be doing the *trian-ri-trian* any hurt! She'll be different to any other bird, and when she'll cry, she'll be lying on her back with her feets lifted up to the sky, and the sky would fall down if she'll not be doing that.'

'Well, I must have a shot at him, even if the firmament were to come about our ears in consequence,' and so saying, our sportsman took his usual kneeling shot and, getting a good and near level, fired; a handful of flying feathers evinced the success of the shot.

The gauger ran to the spot, and Eachainn on the pony trotted after him, but on coming up they could see no bird or evidence of the shot having taken effect. Eachainn looked suddenly aghast.

'What can the gommeril be staring at now?', exclaimed the disappointed gauger.

'Och! Sir,' groaned Eachainn, in great agitation, 'The *Tasg!*, the *Tasg!*'

'The what? You dumbfounded idiot!'

'I'll tell you, sir,' replied the Highlander with great solemnity, 'the *Tasg*, she'll shust be a death bird and the warning'll never fail to come true – 'tis awful, tis shust awful!'

'Well, confound me,' said Gillespie, who was now tired and heated and panting with his exercise, 'Confound me if I can make out the creature. He's no wanting in gumption either, but what havers are these he has got in his noddle?'

Then, addressing his companion, he said, 'Well, now, I have listened to all your nonsense, and now you must tell me in plain words what you mean by all this blether and talk about your *trian-ri-trian* and your *Tasg.*'

To this appeal Eachainn did not reply for some minutes, but dismounting he walked to the very spot where the bird had stood when shot at and picking up the few feathers that had been scattered, stood looking at them with an anxious expression amounting almost to horror. Then turning to the gauger, he replied, in a voice broken with agitation, 'I thocht, sir, that everybody knew that the *Tasg* is a spirit bird, and she'll always be coming to the man who be going to die. She'll come different to peoples. Old Murdo Urquhart, the fisherman, saw her shust like a grey gull and that very night he took ill and died in two or three days. And Barabal, she'll be the bonniest lassie in the place, saw the *Tasg* just like a beautiful white dove and surely poor Barabal, she knew she was going to die, so she made her death shift, and indeed it was very soon she was wearing it. The *Tasg'll* always be coming in the gloamin'; she'll fly low and slow like and she'll no' make any noise with her wings, but if you'll shoot at her, you'll just get nothing but a handful of feather.'

The guide paused a moment, and looking first at the feathers he held in his hand and then in the face of the gauger, he continued, 'I'll be thinking, Sir, that you'll no be living very long. I am just afraid the *Tasg* will be coming to you like a *trian-ri-trian*. Oh, Sir! Indeed I'll be very sorry for you, surely, surely.'

'Look to yourself, man. You say it is my *Tasg*, but I don't see how you make that out; why shouldn't it be your *Tasg* as well as mine?'

'Mine, Sir!' exclaimed Eachainn, 'No, no; I did not shoot her. If you'll shoot her, she'll be your own *Tasg*, surely, and nobody's else, and she'll be just like a *Duine-uasal's Tasg*, a long-legged bird, and she'll just come like the Southeron, at certain times; and then she'll just speak a *craik*, *craik* kind of talk, and that'll no be Gaelic; it'll be the Gaelic that the mavis and the blackbird will be speaking. A lad like me will no get a grand *Tasg* like her. Oh! no, a crow, or a duck, or a *sgarbh* is more like what I'll be getting.'

The gauger, seeing the anxiety of Eachainn to decline the honour of the *Tasg*, was commencing to rally him about it, but in the earnestness of their conversation they had not observed the change which had been gradually taking place in the appearance of the weather; their attention was now, however, called to it by feeling some heavy drops of rain, and they soon saw that a severe storm was looming. They ceased talking and used their breath and energies to better purpose by hurrying forward as fast as they could. In spite of their utmost exertions, the storm soon overtook them, and in half an hour they were both drenched to the skin.

Eachainn took it very philosophically; for this well-developed hardy 'son of the mist' an occasional shower-bath was no hardship. He was too well acquainted with nature in all her changing moods to care much when she frowned. But the poor, town-bred gauger was in a pitiable plight, as he plodded along in a most unenviable state of body and mind, vowing he should catch his death of cold. In about an hour and a half they arrived, to the intense relief of Gillespie, at the hamlet of Dunvegan and gladly availed themselves of the hospitality of *Somhairle Dubh* at the hostelry or change-house of the village.

The worthy hostess of the Dunvegan Hotel met the gauger at the door and dropping a curtsy gave him a hearty welcome, while *Somhairle Dubh* told Eachainn to lead the pony to the stable. Mr Gillespie was shown to his bedroom to change his wet clothes while his dinner was preparing. Before he began his meal, the landlord brought out his own peculiar bottle – a mixture of whisky, camomile flowers, and coriander seeds – and offered his guest a glass as an appetiser, which was gladly accepted, for he was feeling far from well. He ate but little of the good plain dinner provided for him and soon after went to his bed. Before doing so, however, he asked for Eachainn wishing to give him a trifle for his guidance, but on being told that the lad had gone home to his mother, he gave *Somhairle Dubh* a shilling to give him.

Although Gillespie was very tired he could not sleep. He tossed and

turned and only as the day was breaking did he fall asleep, but it did not refresh him for the incidents of his journey haunted him in his sleep. He was again riding the pony, going at a furious rate, while Eachainn sat at his back holding him in a grasp of iron. There arose before him the figure of a snake of gigantic proportions, which, writhing round his neck, was nearly strangling him, but instead of hissing it uttered the *craik, craik* of the *trian-ri-trian*. With an effort he awoke and found himself stiff and feverish and his throat very sore. In a word, the honest man was in for a bad attack of quinsy or inflammation of the throat.

After a few days had elapsed, he expressed his surprise that Eachainn had not called to enquire for him; but he was told the lad had gone to a village ten miles off to lay out his shilling. *Somhairle Dubh* and his good wife became very concerned about their guest, and nothing could exceed their kindness and attention to him. They sent for the doctor, but he was away some distance and could not come at once. On the fourth day of Gillespie's illness, *Somhairle Dubh*, seating himself by the sick man said, with great solemnity of manner, 'Sir, we must all die. Now, Sir, I am come to do to you as I would like to be done by; for sore, sore would it be to me to think my body should not be put in the grave of my father in Kilmuir. So, Sir, by your leave, where would you choose to be buried?'

'Buried!' exclaimed the gauger, aghast, sitting up in his bed and staring at his host. 'Buried! surely I am not so bad as that?'

Without noticing his emotion the worthy man continued, 'Folk have different ways in different countries; but you may depend upon it, Sir, it's no' my father's son that would suffer the corpse of a *Duine-uasal* not to be treated in every way most honourably. You shall be properly washed and stretched – that you may be sure of; and you shall not want for the dead shirt, for by my faith, and I'll do as I promised, Sir, you shall have my own dead shirt that my wife made with her own hands of real good linen, and beautifully sewed too. And we'll keep you, Sir, for the seven days and seven nights, and I'll get *Ian Saor* to make as good a chest for you as ever he made; with brass-headed nails all round it, and with shining handles like silver; and you shall lie in your chest like a *Duine-uasal* should, with two large candles at your head and two at your feet and a plateful of salt on your breast.'

Here poor Gillespie could contain himself no longer but groaned aloud at this dismal recital of what was to be done to his corpse.

'What, Sir? You're maybe thinking the death-feast will not be good enough; but ye need not trouble yourself for that; there shall be plenty whisky and plenty meat, and my wife shall make good bannocks.'

'Yes, indeed I will,' said the good woman, wiping her eyes with her apron as she sobbed out, 'Ochan, ochan! little does his mother know how her son is the night.'

'But,' continued her husband, 'think what a comfort it'll be to her to hear of his being buried so decent-like; for, Sir, you shall be put in my own grandfather's grave, and that's what I'd not do to many, but I'll do it to you, for though you are a gauger you're a stranger far from your own people, and I'd like to show kindness to you.'

The gauger in his weakly state could only lie and moan and in spite of himself become less sceptical and begin to believe that perhaps the corncrake had been a forecast of death after all.

However, the gauger did not die but slowly recovered over the next few weeks due in no small measure to the liberal amounts of whisky that his host fed him – the usual panacea in those days for all evils in the Highlands. We soon find him attending to his duties but making no great attempts to discover the local still that supplied his kind host with the excellent whisky which helped not a little in his recovery. He appeared to do his duty to his King without being unnecessarily harsh with those against whom he was obliged to enforce the law. In short, the gauger and the Highlanders reached an understanding, and they became fast friends.

Adapted from a story by Alistair Og published in *The Celtic Magazine*, 1877.

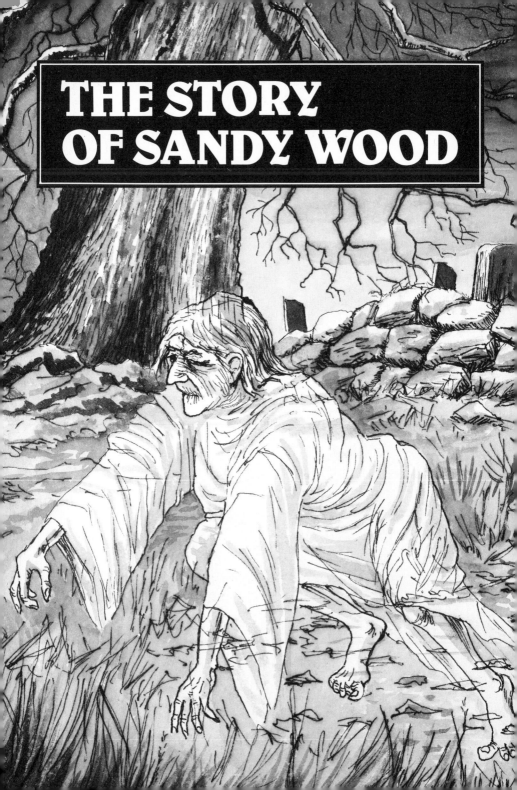

THE STORY OF SANDY WOOD

The Story of Sandy Wood

In the woods to the east of Cromarty, occupying the summit of a green eminence, is the ancient burying-ground and Chapel of St Regulus. The old enclosure of the burying-ground, which seems originally to have been an earthen wall, has now sunk into a grassy mound, and on the southern and western sides large trees – a fine stately ash, fluted like a Grecian column, a huge elm and a low bushy larch with a bent and twisted trunk and weeping branches – spring directly out of it. At one place we see a flat tombstone lying a few yards outside the mound and set apart from the other graves. The near-by trees fling so deep a gloom over it that we can scarcely decipher the epitaph.

To take the trouble to clear away the withered leaves and other debris from the darkened and half-dilapidated inscription will reveal that the tenant below was one Alexander Wood, a native of Cromarty, who died in the year 1690; and that he was interred in this place at his own especial desire. His wife and some of his children have also taken up their places in the graveyard yet none of them are buried close beside him. His story – which, almost too strange for tradition itself, is yet as authentic as most pieces of written history – affords a curious explanation of the circumstances which led him to choose to be buried in this particular spot.

Wood was a man of strong passions, sparingly gifted with common sense, and exceedingly superstitious. No one could be kinder to one's friends or relatives, or more hospitable to a stranger; but when once offended he was implacable. He had but little in his power either as a friend or an enemy – his course through the world lying barely beyond the bleak edge of poverty. If a neighbour, however, dropped in by accident at meal-time, he would not be suffered to quit his house until he had shared with him his simple fare. There was benevolence in the very grasp of his hand and the twinkle of his eye, and the little set speech in which he used to address his wife every time an old or mutilated beggar came to the door is still preserved by tradition: 'Alms, goodwife,' he would say, 'alms to the crippled, and the blind, and the broken-down.'

When injured or insulted, however, and certainly no one could do either without being very much in the wrong, there was a toad-like malignity in his nature that would come leaping out like the reptile from its hole, and no power on earth could shut it up again. He would sit hatching his venom for days and weeks together with a slow, tedious, inoperative kind of perseverance that achieved nothing.

In the house adjoining the one in which he resided, there lived a stout little man, a shoemaker, famous in the village for his great wit and his very considerable knavery. His jokes were mostly practical, and some of the best of them exceedingly akin to felonies. Poor Wood could not understand his wit, but, in his simplicity of heart, he deemed him honest. He knew it, he said, by his very look. Their gardens, like their houses, lay adjoining and were separated from each other, not by a fence, but by four undressed stones laid in a line.

Year after year Wood's garden became less productive; and he had a strange misgiving, but the thing was too absurd to be spoken of, that it was growing smaller every season by the breadth of a whole row of cabbages! On the one side, however, were the back walls of his own and his neighbour's cottages; the four large stones stretched along the other; and nothing, surely, could be less likely than that either the stones or the cottages should take it into their heads to rob him of his property! But the more he strove to exclude the idea the more it pressed upon him. He measured and remeasured to convince himself that it was a false one, and found that he had fallen on just the means of establishing its truth.

The garden was actually growing smaller. But how? Just because it was bewitched! It was shrinking into itself under the force of some potent enchantment. No hypothesis could be more congenial; and he would have held by it, perhaps, until his dying day, had it not been destroyed by one of those chance discoveries which undermine so many beautiful systems and spoil so much ingenious philosophy.

He was lying in bed one morning in spring, about daybreak, when his attention was excited by a strange noise which seemed to come from the garden. Had he heard it two hours earlier, he would have wrapped up his head in the bedclothes and lain still; but now that the cock had crowed, it could not, he concluded, be other than natural. Hastily throwing on part of his clothes, he stole warily to a back window and saw between him and the faint light that was beginning to peep out in the east the figure of a man, armed with a lever, tugging at the stones. Two had already been shifted a full yard nearer the houses, and the figure was straining over a third.

Wood crept stealthily out at the window, crawled on all fours to the intruder, and tripping up his heels, laid him across his lever. It was his knavish neighbour the shoemaker. A scene of noisy contention ensued; groups of half-dressed townsfolk, looming horrible in their shirts and nightcaps through the grey of morning, came issuing through the lanes and the closes; and the combatants were dragged asunder. And well was it for the shoemaker that it happened so; for Wood, though in his sixtieth year, was strong enough and more than angry enough to have torn him to pieces. Now, however, that the warfare had to be carried on by words, the case was quite reversed.

'Neighbours,' said the shoemaker, who had the double advantage of being exceedingly plausible and exceedingly in the wrong, 'I'm desperately ill-used this morning – desperately ill-used – he would both rob me and murder me. I long knew that my wee bit o' yard was growing littler and littler every season; and though no very ready to suspect folk, I just thought I would keep watch and see who was shifting the march-stones. Well, and I did. Late and early did I watch for more than a fortnight; and who did I see this morning through the back window but auld Sandy Wood there in his very shirt – Oh, it's no' him that has any thought o' his end! – poking the stones wi' a long caber into the very heart o' my ground.

'See,' said he, pointing to the ground beside the stones, 'only notice the craft o' the body in tearing up the ground as if they had been moved from my side. Well, I came out and challenged him, as who wouldna'? Says I, "Sandy my man, that's no' honest; I'll no' bear that", and no more had I time to say when up he flew at me like a wildcat, and if it wasna' for yourselves I daresay he would have throttled me. Look how I'm bleeding – and look at him – look at the deceitful body, he hasna' one word to put in for himself.'

There was truth in, at least, this last assertion; for poor Wood, mute with rage and astonishment, stood listening in utter helplessness to the astounding charge of the shoemaker – almost the very charge he himself had to prefer. Twice did he spring forward to grapple with him, but the neighbours held him back, and every time he began to speak his words massed and tangled together and like wreaths of seaweed in a hurricane they stuck in his throat. He continued to rage for three days after, and when the eruption had at last subsided, all his former resentments were found to be swallowed up like the lesser craters of a volcano in the gulf of one immense hatred.

His house, as has been said, lay adjacent to the house of the shoemaker, and he could not avoid seeing him every time he went out or came in – a circumstance which he at first deemed rather gratifying than otherwise. It prevented his hatred from becoming vapid by setting it a' working at least ten times a day, as a musket would a barrel of ale if discharged into the bunghole. Its frequency, however, at length sickened him, and he had employed a mason to build a stone wall, which by stretching from side to side of the close, was to shut out the view, but now he sickened in right earnest and at the end of a few days found himself a' dying.

Still, however, he was possessed by one engrossing resentment. It mingled with all his thoughts of the past and the future; and not only was he to carry it with him to the world to which he was going but also to leave it behind him as a legacy to his children. Among his many other beliefs, there was a superstition handed down from the times of the monks that at the final day of doom all the people of the sheriffdom were to be judged on the Moor of Navity; and both the judgement and the scene of it he had indissolubly associated with the shoemaker and the four stones.

Experience had taught him the importance of securing a first hearing for his story; for was his neighbour, he concluded, to be before him, he would have as slight a chance of being righted at Navity as in his own garden. After brooding over the matter for a whole day, he called his friends and children round his bed and raised himself on his elbow to address them.

'I'm wearing away, bairns and neighbours,' he said, 'and it vexes me sore that that wretched body should see me going afore him. Mind, Jock, that ye'll build the dyke, and make it high, high, and stobbie on the top; and oh! keep him out o' my lykewake [funeral service], for should he but step in at the door, I'll rise, Jock, from the very straiking-board and do murder! Dinna let him so much as look on my coffin. I have been pondering all this day about the meeting at Navity and the march-stones; and I'll tell you, Jock, how we'll match him. Bury me along the saint's dyke on the Navity side, and dinna lay me deep. Ye ken the bonny

green hillock, speckled o'er wi' gowans and puddock-flowers [marsh marigolds] – bury me there, Jock; and I'll get up at the first toot and, I'll wager all I'm worth in the world, I'll be halfway to Navity afore yon short-legged body climbs o'er the dyke.'

Such was the dying injunction of Sandy Wood: and his tombstone still remains to testify that it was religiously attended to.

An Englishman, who came to reside in the parish nearly an age after and to whom the story must have been imparted in a rather imperfect manner, was shocked by what he deemed this unfair plot. The litigants, he said, should start together; he was certain it would be so in England where a fair field was all that would be given to St Dunstan himself though he fought with the Devil. And that it might be so here, he buried the tombstone of Wood under an immense heap of clay and gravel. It would keep him down, he said, until the little fellow would have clambered over the wall. The townsfolk, however, who were better acquainted with the merits of the case, shovelled the heap aside, and it now forms the two little hillocks which overtop the stone.

A traditional tale of Cromarty, first published in 1869 in *Scenes and Legends* by Hugh Miller.

RODERICK MACKENZIE

Roderick Mackenzie

Culloden was the last battle fought on British soil. The last battle in a civil war between those who supported the Hanoverian King George and those who sought to restore the Stuarts to the throne. For the Jacobites, as the Stuart supporters were called, the battle was a tragic disaster. They fought a set-piece encounter against superior forces on ground ill-suited to the clansmen's style of attack. The result was the rout of the Highland army. This not only meant the end of the Stuart cause but also the end of an ancient civilisation and the devastation of the countryside.

The Jacobite forces were led by Prince Charles Edward Stuart, the son of the exiled King James. He had led them as far south as Derby and had defeated the Hanoverians in a series of battles but now, after his army's decisive defeat at Culloden, he and many of those who had fought for his cause became fugitives to be hunted down by the redcoat soldiers of the Hanoverian army. Charles sought refuge in the islands of the Hebrides.

Fort Augustus lies at the south-west end of Loch Ness and stands upon a narrow strip of land formed by the River Tarff on one side and the River Oich on the other. This fort, built in 1727 by General Wade, was one of a string of Hanoverian forts built throughout the length of the Great Glen. The fort had been captured and destroyed at the end of February 1746 by a detachment of the Prince's army, but a few days after their victory at Culloden the Hanoverian army reoccupied it. Because of the severe damage, done to it by the Highlanders, they were only able to use part of it as cells in which to keep their Jacobite prisoners.

In the fields near the fort row upon row of tents were pitched to accommodate the eleven battalions that had marched there from Inverness. An advance party of three brigades together with eight companies of Argyle Militia arrived on 16 May and they were joined a week later by the rest of the army, led by the Duke of Cumberland. It was intended that they would stay on at Fort Augustus for six weeks, this being the length of time Cumberland thought would be necessary to crush all signs of resistance in the area.

Every day redcoats left Fort Augustus to patrol far and wide over the whole of the Western Highlands. Some were large parties of one or two hundred men; others were small patrols. Each man drew enough bread and cheese, and powder and ball for a week's march into the hostile countryside. They went not only to burn and plunder but also to search for the Prince, for it was rumoured that he had returned to the mainland from the Western Isles. The soldiers searched diligently for they stood to gain a reward of £30,000 for his capture. The larger parties of redcoats would have had a full complement of officers and NCOs, but the small patrols, sometimes consisting of only six men, were under the command of a sergeant or a corporal.

One day towards the middle of July one such patrol was in Glenmoriston when it happened to see a young man by the name of Roderick Mackenzie. Roderick was a fugitive for he had served as an officer in the Prince's army. Since Culloden he had roamed the hills of the central Highlands, unable to return to his home in Edinburgh where his father owned a jewellery business. A Jacobite gentleman returning to that city after fighting in the Prince's army would have faced immediate arrest. There was a large garrison of Hanoverian troops there, and many of the civilian population supported the Hanoverian King.

Roderick had reached a spot between Aonach and Ceannacroc when, on turning a bend in the road, he saw a redcoat patrol of six men. The soldiers also had seen him and they called upon him to stand, but Roderick turned and ran as fast as his legs would carry him. Unluckily for Roderick, the soldiers' muskets were primed and ready to fire, for such a small party was nervous of possible attack by hostile clansmen. They fired at him and, hit in the back by a musket ball, he fell mortally wounded. The redcoats ran forward and stood looking down at him as his blood drained away into the heather.

'He's got red hair,' said one of the redcoats, a North Country Englishman, as he stooped down to remove the bonnet from Roderick's head. 'He's abaht right built too.'

The soldier had addressed the remark to the Sergeant in charge of the patrol who said, 'If tha thinks tha going ta get reward thad better think again; does tha think he'd be travellin' alone?'

Roderick lay still, allowing the redcoats to believe that he was dead. A dreadful pain in his chest was beginning to replace the strange dull ache which he had at first experienced. This and the high-pitched whine in his ears told him that he would soon be dead. But he did not care any longer. Already he felt detached from his body and from life as he had known it. He had heard and understood the redcoats' conversation. They believed that he might be the Prince, and he realised then that there was perhaps one last service he could perform. It took an effort of will for him to raise his eyelids, but finally he succeeded. He saw only a blur of red uniforms as though far away. A trickle of blood ran from his mouth as he whispered, 'You . . . You have killed your Prince!'

The soldiers heard and stood staring at the body for several seconds before turning to look at one another with open mouths. The expressions on their faces revealed that perhaps, after all, this was the Prince.

'I told yer it were 'im, Sergeant,' said the first soldier excitedly.

'Ay well, yer can't take his word for it,' said the Sergeant, unwilling to allow himself to believe that he was now a very rich man, but secretly nothing in the world would have stopped him taking that body back to the fort and staking his claim to the reward money.

'He looks like 'im,' said a third soldier, moving closer. 'Red hair and fat-faced. Bloody hell! It's worth takin' im back ta find out anyway up!'

'Ay well, tha can carry 'im then,' said the first soldier.

'Naybody need carry 'im,' said the sergeant. 'All wi need for identification is his head.'

'Ay, t'sergeant's right. If we'd taken 'im alive that's how he'd have ended up anyhow – wihaht 'is head,' said the third soldier, laughing.

'Well, come on then,' said the Sergeant, addressing the third soldier. 'Tha can do't carvin'.'

The soldier drew his hanger from its sheath and kneeling beside the body began to hack away at the neck. Roderick Mackenzie had not lived to know that his ruse had been successful. He no longer heard nor felt anything. The Sergeant stood watching the operation for a few seconds before suddenly remembering that they would still have the body to dispose of. Turning to the others he said, 'Find a place ta get rid o't body.'

'Why not shove it in't river, Sergeant,' suggested one of them, with a thought to saving himself the work of digging a grave.

'Nay, they might want ta look it ower, so we'd best hide it in a place where we can find it again,' replied the Sergeant.

The soldiers turned away and began to search for a spot where they could bury the body without too much effort on their part. Meanwhile the head had been successfully removed, and the soldier who had carried out the task stood holding it by the hair as he bent to wipe the blade of his hanger on a grassy bank.

The Sergeant said, 'Gi' me t'head. It needs ta be washed.' So saying, he took hold of the gory object and carried it across the road and down to the river bank where he swirled it about in the gently flowing water. The other soldiers were shouting from further along the bank that they had found a suitable spot for the body, and the Sergeant called to them to drag the body there. When he was satisfied with the condition of the head he joined the others. They had laid the body beneath an overhanging grass bank and were now stamping down the turf with their boots. When the job was completed and they were assembling on the road to begin the march back to Fort Augustus, they congratulated each other on their good fortune and discussed how they would spend the reward money.

Meanwhile, in one of the ground-floor cells at Fort Augustus lay Alexander MacDonald of Kingsburgh in the Isle of Skye, accused of having concealed the Prince for three days on that island. The room in which he was confined was without windows, and he spent most of the time in total darkness. There was a piece of tallow candle on the table in the centre of the room but this remained unlit unless his gaolers thought fit to light it when they brought him his food. The cell was as cold as the grave even on the warmest of days because of the great thickness of masonry between it and the outside world. His bed was a pile of straw in one corner of the red-brick floor. Although the fort was for the most part built of the local stone, the floor, walls and vaulted ceiling of the room were lined with these red bricks baked by the army's sappers from the clay on the shores of Loch Ness.

Hour after hour, day after day, Kingsburgh lay in that dark cell not knowing whether it be day or night; sometimes dropping into a fitful sleep only to be awakened from it, time and again, by the ring and scrape of ammunition boots upon the flagstones in the passage outside his door. This passage, leading from the main entrance of the fort to the central barrack square, had two cells on either side. It was the only substantial part of the fort left undamaged. The Highlanders had set charges and blown up much of the structure after they had captured the place in February.

One morning in July the monotony of Kingsburgh's days had been broken by the shouts of his gaolers and the rattle of keys as they unlocked all the cells in the passage and ordered the prisoners out. Puzzled by this, Kingsburgh stumbled out into the brightly lit passage with his eyes screwed up and covered by a hand against the light. Prisoners from the other cells were standing in the passage and beyond them stood the officer of the guard holding a sheet of paper in his hand.

The officer spoke. 'The following prisoners are to be released.' He then read a short list of names from the paper. One of the names was that of Alexander MacDonald. This was Kingsburgh's name, but he could not believe that he was the Alexander MacDonald named in the document. After the others on the list had stepped forward the officer again called the name and then asked Kingsburgh if that were not his name.

He answered, 'That is my name, but I suspect there must be some mistake.'

'Damn you! What mistake?' said the officer, 'Is not your name Alexander MacDonald?'

'It is,' replied Kingsburgh, 'but I doubt if I am the one referred to on your list.'

Despite Kingsburgh's protests he soon found himself outside the fort and a free man. In the village street he met a friend who advised him to leave the area at once, but Kingsburgh said, 'No; I must wait at the alehouse opposite till I see whether the officer gets into a scrape.' He waited there two hours until he heard that an officer had gone with a body of troops to arrest the subaltern on guard for having set at large so dangerous a rebel. Kingsburgh immediately ran across the street and, saying to the officer 'There, I told you there was a mistake,' surrendered himself.

On the face of it this seems to be very strange behaviour on Kingsburgh's part. No doubt he was seriously concerned lest the young subaltern should suffer on his account, for this was the nature of the man, but also he knew that as soon as the mistake was discovered search-parties would immediately be sent out to apprehend him once more. He had originally been arrested on Skye, but such was his reputation as a man of honour that he was given his parole to take himself to Fort Augustus unescorted, which he did, arriving there at the beginning of July.

Kingsburgh had only been returned to the idleness of confinement a few days when a senior officer approached him with the question, 'Would you know the Young Pretender's head if you saw it?'

'I would know the head very well if it were on the shoulders,' replied Kingsburgh.

'But what if the head be not on the shoulders – do you think you should know it in that case?'

'In that case, I will not pretend to know anything about it,' said Kingsburgh.

Since other prisoners at Fort Augustus had answered in the same vein, the authorities were frustrated in their attempt to positively identify the severed head of Roderick Mackenzie as that of the Prince. The Duke of Cumberland, who was preparing to depart for London, decided that the head must travel with him, and in order to preserve it for the journey the soldiers thought to immerse it in brine. The Duke left the fort on Friday, 18 July, the head among his baggage. Three of his aides rode with him together with a Captain's Escort of Kingston's Horse.

When he reached the north of England the Duke sent a message to the garrison commander at Carlisle ordering him to despatch to London under escort one of the Jacobite prisoners held by him, namely Richard Morison who had been Valet-de-chambre to Prince Charles. When the Duke's baggage arrived in the capital, a week after it had left Fort Augustus, the head of Roderick Mackenzie was sent to Southwark Gaol where Richard Morison was, but when the head was unpacked it was found to be too badly decomposed for the purposes of identification.

Word of the possible death of the Prince and the claim for the reward spread to all the military garrisons in Scotland, and for a week or two the soldiers became less energetic in their search for the Prince.

Many years later a stone cairn was erected at the lonely spot in Glenmoriston where Roderick Mackenzie died, and on the riverbank nearby his grave was marked by a simple wooden cross. Today that cairn still stands and the grave is still marked by a wooden cross. Each time the cross has rotted away it has been replaced by those who find time, even in this modern age, to honour a hero of a long-lost cause.

As Sure as Death

Many in the Scottish Highlands live far from the main centres of human habitation and have no alternative but to rely on their own resources or on their neighbours' in dealing with sickness and death. This was particularly true in the past when bad roads and primitive transport added to their difficulties. Every glen had individuals who had acquired a reputation for being in possession of one skill or another. Although not professionally qualified, these amateurs would serve the community by performing the duties of veterinary, midwife, doctor and undertaker.

Although the need for such self-sufficiency has lessened in recent years owing to improved communications, it has not entirely disappeared. Some of the palliatives, methods and practices used by these amateur practitioners would no doubt be considered strange by those living in the more densely populated areas. Nevertheless, where the services of the professional are not readily available, these people do perform a necessary function, very often most efficiently and with good results. However, there are times when the efficacy of some of the treatments and the accuracy of some of the diagnoses are highly doubtful.

I once read somewhere about a young man who was treated for severe colic by one of these amateur medical practitioners. Despite the ministrations of this person, the patient's condition failed to improve. He lingered on in agonising pain for some time and, after great suffering, appeared to have died. After his remains were interred in the churchyard a young woman, to whom he had plighted his troth and whom he was to marry, felt the death of her lover so deeply that she made a pilgrimage to the burial-place the day after his interment.

The sorrowing maiden heard groans coming from beneath the newly laid turf, a circumstance which both awed and terrified her. She lost no time in telling her story to the relatives, and they lost still less in setting about opening the grave. When the lid of the coffin was removed, to their astonishment and horror they found that the body had turned and was lying face downwards. After thoroughly satisfying themselves that their relative was now truly dead, the corpse was reverently adjusted in its resting-place.

This was supposed to have happened a long time ago, but much more recently a friend of mine, a city-dweller, told me of an experience he had which might have led to someone being buried alive. He told me the story when we were seated before a blazing log fire with a bottle of good malt whisky between us, pleasantly passing a long Highland winter evening telling one another tall stories. This story, however, he swore was true in every detail; in fact, he stressed this by using a popular Highland expression, 'It's true, as sure as death.' So now I shall set down the story just as he told it to me.

I had only recently come to live in the Highlands after having spent the first forty years of my life in the big city. Although I was rapturously happy in this new location, I was totally unfamiliar with Highland ways and this meant that I was constantly being introduced to new and strange experiences.

The village in which I had come to live was far from any town. It had a shop which stocked most essentials, but only the essentials. But one thing the village did have, and that was a blacksmith's shop. I have always been fascinated by rural craftsmen at work, and so I became a regular visitor to the smithy. There were, in fact, two blacksmiths employed there, the brothers Hughie and George Mackenzie. They were interesting characters and I spend a lot of time with them. Being from the city where people have little time for one another I found their willingness to linger in conversation with a stranger somewhat surprising. Later I would grow used to their ways and I, too, would learn to live at a slower pace.

'The two brothers were obviously finding things increasingly difficult in their trade, not only because there was now less work for blacksmiths, but also because they had become too old for the job, although they refused to admit this, even to themselves. They told me of the many changes that they had seen in the glen. How once there had been hundreds of horses employed on the farms, crofts and in the forests dragging timber, but now few people owned horses.

They were both small men and bent with age, although stockily built and with the strong arms and hands of the blacksmith. Hughie was the younger and fitter of the two, and although he was deaf, his deafness was not nearly as bad as that of his brother George. Hughie had wit and sagacity, and he possessed a great fund of amusing stories. These were all taken from real life and he loved to relate them. However, his memory was beginning to fail him and he would often repeat a story, forgetting that he had told it only a short time before. I didn't mind this because, like a child listening to a familiar fairy-story, I would take pleasure in noticing changes or omissions in the tales he told.

Neither of the brothers had married. They lived together in a small cottage beside the smithy with their two sisters, both ancient like themselves. Whilst Hughie ran the business Jane, the younger of the two sisters, had complete control of their domestic arrangements. Jane was a small, stout woman: so small, she could not have been more than four feet six inches tall, whereas her sister, Joan, was of normal build and slimmer, too. She was also the eldest in the family and her health was failing. Every winter she would have to take to her bed for weeks at a time, and when I would visit them to sit by the fire in the kitchen talking, I would hear her moaning and groaning as she lay in bed in the small room next door. Because the three old people were each of them deaf to some degree, I would often wonder if they failed to hear her, or if they just pretended not to hear. Sometimes between the moaning and the groaning she would suddenly give a heart-stopping shriek. I remember the first time this happened I was quite alarmed and expressed my concern to Jane, but she reassured me saying, 'She has terrible nightmares', and ever after that I ignored the sounds just as they did.

As the weather improved each year so did the health of the old lady and usually on the first warm day of spring she would be on her feet again and as cheerful and lucid as she had been before winter's cold had laid her low. Her annual winter hibernation continued during the first few years of my stay in the village, and I came to accept it as normal, just as the family did.

'About four years later I happened to be at the smithy one winter's day when a lorry delivered a number of rough planks of wood, each about six feet long and perhaps six inches in width. Hughie put them into the smithy, but he didn't stow them away among the untidy clutter of things which almost filled that building. Instead he leaned them up against one of the workbenches, as if he intended to make use of them quite soon. When I went into the smithy a few days later I saw that the planks were still standing there. I grew curious about these planks and tried to think what use he might have for them. They were in the way when either Hughie or George worked at the bench, but they made no effort to move them, and I thought it strange that they should work round them even though it was obviously inconvenient for them to do so. I could have asked them what use they intended for the planks but because they didn't volunteer this information, I somehow felt that they didn't want me to ask.

'The lights in the smithy cottage always burned late into the night. Being old, the smithy folk were inclined to doze off at odd intervals during the day so I suppose they didn't require much sleep at night. Consequently, they seldom retired before the early hours, but even so the smoke from their chimney was always the first to be seen next morning. I am something of a night owl myself and so I would often call on them late at night. On one of these late night visits in mid-winter, when a heavy frost was on the ground, I noticed a strange atmosphere in the cottage. There was something different about Hughie's greeting when he answered the door and when I entered the kitchen, although George was seated in his usual place by the fire, gazing fixedly at the coals, he didn't look up. I thought that perhaps he hadn't heard me enter. Jane, standing by the table in the middle of the room, gave me a half-smile. Something was wrong: but what? Then Jane said 'Joan has gone. She went a few minutes ago at about eleven forty-five.' She said this so casually that at first I didn't understand. I thought that perhaps she meant Joan had been taken to hospital or had left the house for some other destination. But then it dawned on me. Joan had died. I offered my condolences and I must have looked very sad because Jane said quickly, 'She went peacefully in her sleep. She is better off . . . the weather was too cold for her.'

'Yes,' I said, 'the weather is cold, and if she didn't suffer. . . .'

'Grannie and Mrs Noble are washing her now,' said Jane. 'They're good neighbours: Very good neighbours; but they won't be able to lift her.'

'Lift her?', said I stupidly.

'She'll have to be laid out,' said Jane with authority.

'Of course,' I agreed, still not understanding the full implications.

'Throughout my conversation with Jane I had been aware of Hughie standing close behind me. I could hear his rasping breath and I knew that he would be leaning forward, his hand to his ear, intent on hearing every word of our conversation. I felt a tug on my sleeve and turned to look at him. He continued to pull at my sleeve until he had manœuvred me into a corner of the room. His manner told me that he had something of a confidential nature to impart. He whispered, 'How would ye like to make something for me?'

'Er . . . make something?' I asked, puzzled.

'Aye, yer good wi' yer hands and I'm sure ye could make a job o'it,' said Hughie in the same conspiratorial whisper. My mind raced trying to imagine what he could possibly want me to make for him, and why it should be a secret, and why he should ask me to make it at nearly midnight with his sister lying dead in the next room. I managed to say, 'Of course, anything I can do to help.'

'A mortboard!' announced Hughie his eyes a'twinkle as if he had announced something of great import.

I was still as much in the dark as before. A what-board? I asked myself. Hughie could see that I was puzzled and this seemed to give him pleasure for he twinkled all the more.

'She'll need to be laid out,' declared Hughie, repeating what his sister had already stressed.

'Yes,' I agreed but without understanding. Then Hughie chose to put me out of my misery by being more explicit. He said, 'We'll put the mortboard between two chairs in the room; then we'll lay her on it nice and flat. I have the wood in the smithy.'

Hughie gave me a key and I went out into the dark and frosty night and let myself into the smithy. I found the wood lying in the place where it had rested for the past week and I wondered how they could have known in advance that a mortboard would shortly be required. To me it had seemed that the old lady's health had been no worse this winter than in any previous year.

The planks had been soaking wet when delivered, and I now found them encrusted with ice and solidly frozen together. In separating them one from another and in handling them while making the mortboard, my hands became numb with cold. By the time I had the job completed my whole body was almost in the same condition.

I carried the heavy board to the cottage with hands that had no feeling, and Hughie helped me set it up in the room at the opposite end of the cottage from the kitchen. This room was unheated and the vapour of our breath hung in the cold air. We placed the mortboard on the seats of two dining-chairs and covered it with a white sheet. Before returning to the kitchen Hughie took a bottle of whisky from a cupboard in the room, giving me a mischievous wink as he did so. We went into the kitchen where he poured generous amounts of the whisky into three glasses. One for me and one each for George and himself.

A few minutes later we were joined by the two ladies who had been washing the corpse. These capable women, mother and daughter, were neighbours and they were always called in by the locals when there was a death. I had learned that, although always ready to participate in their neighbours' joys, Highlanders on such occasions as this are equally ready to share in their sorrows and will not grudge to contribute their assistance, by night as well as by day.

After our break for refreshments the younger of the two ladies, a small stout woman of a jolly disposition (a useful attribute in her line of work) explained to me that the body would have to be carried into the end room so that it could be laid out. This, she said, would have to be done at once, before rigor mortis set in, for if the body should set in its present bent position the undertaker would have difficulty getting it into the coffin. She further explained that the moving of the body would have to be done by one person alone because of the confined spaces in the bedroom and the fact that there were three doorways to be negotiated. As all this was being explained to me I nodded my head from time to time to show that I understood. But what I didn't at first understand was that she expected me to carry the body. When the full realisation of this came to me I knew that I had been too hasty in agreeing so readily, and I immediately began to think up some alternative arrangement. But it was too late. They were all looking at me expectantly, waiting for me to make a move.

I shot a glance at the half-empty whisky bottle standing on the table among the tea-cups and I fought off a strong urge to grab it and drain its contents at a gulp. The ladies were moving towards the bedroom door and I found myself following them. They were willing me to move the body and I was helpless to resist.

I stood in the bedroom and looked down on poor Joan. Her cheeks were more deeply sunken than I remembered them having been. She was paler too; but otherwise she could have been sleeping. Then a sudden panicky thought struck me. What if she wasn't dead. If I carried her into that icy, cold room and laid her on those ice-covered boards she would surely die then. 'Has the doctor seen her?' I asked.

'The doctor saw her yesterday,' said the stout lady, 'and he told them that he didn't expect her to last the night.'

'But shouldn't he see her now?' I asked, 'I mean, for the death certificate?'

'Och, she's gone alright,' said the little woman confidently, 'I made sure o' that. I held a mirror to her face. Och aye, she's gone alright. It's too late and too far for the doctor to be coming. He'll send the certificate down on the first bus. He's very good like that!'

I realised that she meant that the doctor would issue a death certificate without ever seeing the deceased. My mind boggled, and I began wondering how many people had been buried alive because their family and neighbours had thought that they were dead when perhaps they were only in a deep coma. But then, I reasoned, perhaps this business with the death certificate only happens when the person concerned is very old. Or, was it only when the deceased lived too far from the doctor's house? Or, perhaps, this sort of thing only happened on cold winter's nights when the roads were icy and it was dangerous for the doctor to travel? Or, could it possibly be (perish the thought!) that if someone phoned the doctor and told him that you were dead, he would send a certificate down on the first bus because 'He's very good like that!'

The stout little lady was becoming impatient with me. I had been standing there for sometime while these nightmarish thoughts flitted through my troubled mind, so now she pushed in front of me and began to demonstrate how I should lift the body. She said 'If you put one arm under her shoulder-blades and the other under her knees you will be able to get her through the door no bother.'

It all sounded so sensible and easy. After all, I reasoned, the doctor had been satisfied that she was close to death; and she was old; and she had been sick for a long time, and my advisers had far more experience of death than I had. Thus, I succeeded in convincing myself that I should move the body.

When I put my arms under the old lady I was surprised at the warmth I felt, and doubt began to creep back into my mind. Then, as I began to raise her from the bed, as instructed, she let out a moan. No, it was more of a croak, but quite enough to give me a nasty turn. I felt the blood drain from my head and I let the body sink back onto the bed.

'It's only air in her lungs,' said the little woman reassuringly.

'Yes, of course,' said I, in a voice I didn't recognise.

I tried again, and this time managed to ignore the odd sound of exhaled air. I carried the body sideways through the bedroom doorway and into the kitchen, where the watching family made me feel strangely

142

embarrassed. They seemed to take the whole thing quite casually, as though it was an everyday occurrence. Was it because they were old and close to death? Or was it because they were Highlanders that they were able to accept this macabre scene?

After placing the body on the mortboard I left the two ladies to their job of laying-out and gratefully returned to the warmth of the kitchen and there calmed my frayed nerves with a generous helping of whisky from Hughie's bottle.

After this experience of rural living I seriously considered moving house once again, preferably to a part of the country where a death certificate would be less likely to arrive by the first bus.

ISBN 0-7117-0532-1
© 1985 William Owen
Published by Jarrold Publishing, Norwich
Printed in Great Britain. 4/90